The Day Job

Mark Wallington was born in Swanage in Dorset in 1953. He worked for a while as a gardener in London before becoming a scriptwriter and a journalist. In 1982 he walked the South West Coastal Path and his subsequent book, *500-Mile Walkies*, became a bestseller. In 1992 Mark Wallington published his novel *The Missing Postman* and then wrote the script for the award-winning television play starring James Bolam. He is much sought-after as a film and television writer, working from his home in the High Peak in Derbyshire, where he keeps a truly wonderful garden. He is married with two children.

ALSO BY MARK WALLINGTON

500-Mile Walkies
Destination Lapland
Boogie Up the River
Pennine Walkies
The Missing Postman
Happy Birthday, Mr Shakespeare

The Day Job

ADVENTURES OF A
JOBBING GARDENER

MARK WALLINGTON

arrow books

Published by Arrow Books in 2006

16

First published in the United Kingdom by Hutchinson in 2005

Arrow Books
Tha Random House Group Limited
20 Vauxhall Bridge Road, London SW1V 2SA

www.randomhouse.co.uk

Addresses for companies within The Random House Group Limited can be found
at: www.randomhouse.co.uk/offices.htm

The Random House Group Limited Reg. No. 954009

A CIP catalogue record for this book
is available from the British Library

ISBN 9780099472674

Penguin Random House is committed to a sustainable future for
our business, our readers and our planet. This book is made from
Forest Stewardship Council® certified paper.

Printed and bound in Great Britain by Clays Ltd, Elcograf S.p.A.

For My Mother

CONTENTS

WINTER

SPRING

1

MRS FLEMING

Mrs Fleming lived down the hill from Hampstead Pond in a big house with dirty windows, a house that stood out in the neighbourhood because it didn't have a blue plaque on the wall — George Orwell had never been a tenant; Karl Marx had never sat in the garden.

I stood on the doorstep, panting. I'd cycled up steep hills out of the bowels of the city to this desirable place where the air was cool and the rain was warm. I composed myself and rang the bell, wondering if I should affect an accent, something rustic, something from the West Country perhaps.

The door opened and there was a woman with long silver hair piled up on her head in a nest. She was wearing a pair of trousers with pads stitched to the knees, and from her belt hung a ring of keys that made her look like a jailer.

'What are you doing here?' she said. I noticed she was holding a knife and fork in her hand.

'I'm . . . the gardener,' I announced. It was the first time

I had said that to anyone and I felt a wave of guilt wash over me.

'Did you ring the bell?'

'Yes.'

'It doesn't work . . . I was looking for my lunch.'

She looked from side to side around the little paved front courtyard. I looked as well, but there was no sign of any lunch.

'I put it down somewhere,' she sighed. 'It's always disappearing.'

She led me into the house, and I immediately understood how someone could lose their lunch in here. Each room was darkened with assorted piles of clutter. It was hard to turn a corner without toppling something. Stacks of books wobbled as one manoeuvred past. Shelves sagged under the weight of boxes and tins. A bicycle wheel hung from a hook where a picture might once have been. Furniture sat on top of other furniture. Everywhere were parcels of newspapers. A stuffed animal – an otter perhaps – crouched in a glass cabinet.

Then there, on a pile of *National Geographic*, I spied a plate with two crackers, a lump of blue cheese and a pickled onion. 'Look!' I said, rather pleased with myself.

She looked, but screwed up her face. 'That's not it.'

We passed through what was probably the living room. A TV stood on a trunk, an overflowing waste-paper basket perched on it. Behind it the mantelpiece was crammed with empty bottles. In the middle of the room was a chair with an open book on it.

'It's a puzzle,' said Mrs Fleming. 'I was reading a play by Tom Stoppard . . . do you like Tom Stoppard?'

This could have been a trick question, the one she asked all prospective employees. Get the answer wrong and you weren't hired.

'To a point,' I said.

'I think he's the best playwright we have.'

'Yes.'

'. . . And I got up to find my *History of the Napoleonic Wars*, and when I got back to the chair . . . my lunch was gone.'

'I see.'

'It'll turn up. It always does. Eventually. The garden's this way.'

She went through into the kitchen, fighting her way through sails of drying laundry. She said to me, 'I telephoned you because now that I've got the house in order I'm going to turn my attention to the garden.'

She slipped her feet into some white wellingtons, then with one of the keys from her chain she unlocked the back door.

There, waiting on the doorstep, was a tortoise.

'Ah Jasper,' said Mrs Fleming. 'Say hello to Jasper.'

'Hello Jasper,' I said and wondered if you stroked tortoises.

'You need to keep your eye on Jasper. He gets depressed.'

Mrs Fleming's garden looked like the last piece of wilderness in Britain. Once, long ago, there might have been some sort of design to it, but now it lay like a sleeping beauty, lost under ancient towering shrubs and knotted beds. The lawn was a duvet of moss. The shed had lichen for a roof. Creepers had wrapped themselves around every angle and made a bid for next door. It was a jungle of neglect. It was quite frightening.

Mrs Fleming gestured grandly. 'I have great plans. But . . . before we do anything I want to put you to a little test.'

A test. Oh how I had dreaded those words. I wondered whether I should just turn and run, because the truth was, although I had advertised myself as a gardener, although that morning I had dressed carefully in the style I thought suitable for a gardener – corduroys, checked shirt, old Hush Puppies – and although, as I surveyed the overgrown beds, I was stroking my chin in the manner I imagined a gardener would, the truth was my knowledge of the activity was slim. Basic, in fact. I could dig things up, I could cut things back, I could mow a lawn and I could build a bonfire, but for anything more creative – anything that leaned towards cultivation – I would have to consult a manual. My plan was to learn on the job. My problem was I needed a job in the first place. The last thing I wanted was a test.

Mrs Fleming grabbed a trowel and led me down the garden path, past a tree with a pink blossom I didn't know the name of; past a screen of shrubs not one of which I could identify; past a climbing thing with a black mould on its leaves that I had no idea how to eradicate.

She pointed into the undergrowth. 'See in there . . . ?'

My spirits rose. She was pointing in the direction of the only clump of flowers in the garden I could identify – bluebells. 'Yes.'

'That's where we buried Stanley.'

She continued on to the bottom where the lawn ended in a tangle of brambles. She said, 'I think I'd like to have a sort of Japanese garden here.'

'Japanese, right you are,' I nodded. 'I'll make a note.'

'And there's the rockery, look. I would love to see it restored to its former glory.'

It would have needed an archaeological dig to restore the rockery to its former glory.

'Restore rockery. Leave it to me,' I said.

The path turned a right angle past the shed – which might have been nineteenth-century – and Mrs Fleming came to an abrupt stop. 'Ah. Here we are,' and she pointed down to a dandelion sitting happily in a big crack in the path. 'Do you know what that is?'

I looked at her carefully. I wanted to say: I never meant to mislead you, I really didn't. I just thought I could be useful mowing or raking leaves. All I really want is to work outside for the summer.

'It's . . . a dandelion.'

'Good. Now. I want you to dig it up for me,' and she handed me the trowel.

'Is this the test?'

'Yes. I don't like dandelions.'

I didn't know if there was a right or a wrong way to dig up a dandelion, but I plunged that trowel in so deep and whipped the roots out so fast it never felt a thing.

I stood there, clutching the already limp corpse, wondering what I should do with it. I couldn't just throw it over my shoulder. What did gardeners do with weeds? Maybe they took them home. 'I don't like dandelions either,' I said, and popped it in my pocket.

Mrs Fleming looked at me carefully now. She had wild eyes to match her wild hair. It occurred to me she was the kind of person you tried not to sit next to in a public place. She said, 'Can you come on Tuesdays?'

'Tuesdays are fine.'

'Nine thirty to eleven thirty.'

'Perfect.'

'You can have a cup of coffee at ten thirty.'

'Thank you.'

'With a biscuit . . . if I can find the tin.'

She laughed at her own joke. I laughed with her, and I felt a burst of confidence. I could do this job. I could be a gardener.

2

MISS CLARA

Gardening would be my day job, that was the plan. It would support me until I was able to make a living from writing.

Quite how I would ever make a living from writing was another matter. At the age of twenty-six I was still waiting for my first break. 'Just write one of those books by Jackie Collins!' Mandy the hairdresser who lived downstairs said to me. But I'd already tried that and stopped at the bottom of page 1. I'd stopped at the bottom of page 1 of a couple of plays as well. I'd tried short stories but they were always too long. My epic poems came up too short. I'd fooled around with song lyrics. I'd dabbled with journalism. I was stuck.

Then one morning I visited the doctor, and there in the waiting room I saw where my future lay.

Sitting opposite me was a man wearing a lumpy raincoat and checked cap. He was flicking through *Autocar*, and he wheezed regularly as he tapped his feet to a tune in his head. He was just asking to be a character in something. But not a novel, or a play. He wasn't for a poem either, or a song.

He was, without doubt, perfect material for a three-minute television sketch for *The Two Ronnies*.

He coughed, but I wasn't fooled, there was nothing wrong with him. He was a salesman in human organs working the black market. When he got in to see the doctor he would flash open his coat and there would hang an assortment of items for transplant: kidneys, hearts, corneas, all well below market price. 'Want some bone marrow, Doc? Got some fresh in from Holland, on special.'

I went home and turned him into a three-minute sketch. Ronnie Corbett would play him; Ronnie Barker would be the doctor. I wrote it in minutes and sent it off. The Two Ronnies sent it back almost as quickly.

But then I showed it to my friend Dick. He took a long look at it. He laughed in all the right places. Then he handed it back to me and said it was rubbish, adding that he thought we should become a writing team.

'Your material needs beefing up, that's all,' he said.

'What do you mean beefing up?'

'It's too . . . mainstream. How about making the salesman an alien?'

Aliens featured a lot in Dick's writing, but I could cope with that. I thought we complemented each other well. We would each benefit from a partnership: Dick had all the jokes, and I had a typewriter. So from then on our evenings and weekends were spent together in a room writing comedy. We sent off our sketches with stamped addressed envelopes and they came back with rejection letters. Some producers were encouraging, others told us to stop wasting our time, but as long as we made each other laugh we were keen to continue, convinced success would come sooner or later. We just needed time to write and enough money to support ourselves. Dick worked in a pub on Hackney Marshes where he also had accommodation, and I worked for a van-driving agency which earned me enough to pay for a room in a first-floor flat owned by a mortgage broker named Neil.

But now it was April. That sweet, sickly smell in the air was spring battling with the traffic fumes. The prospect of being stuck in a van in London for the summer didn't appeal at all, so I put a postcard in a newsagent's window in Hampstead: 'Spring is here! Gardener available for all aspects of garden maintenance. £1.50 an hour.'

I showed it to Neil: he laughed. I showed it to Mandy downstairs: she laughed. I showed it to Dick, and he laughed longest and hardest. In fact, he said it was the funniest thing I'd written since we'd been working together.

Mrs Fleming had phoned almost as soon as I returned home from placing the advert. But she was an enigma, always likely to do the opposite to everyone else. I wrote her name on my calendar, then waited for the other days to fill up, but, other than a man who phoned to ask if I repaired lawn-mowers, she was my only response.

Word of mouth would do the trick! I told myself. I just needed to get working, get my face seen around the herbaceous borders of Hampstead and Highgate. So I gave Mrs Fleming's wilderness all my attention that first week. She seemed happy to let me come on Tuesday and every other morning as well. I hacked away at her beds and cut out her dead wood. I pulled things up and dug things out. It occurred to me I was a purely destructive gardener, but I could see a positive side to that. I thought: destruction is what I can specialise in.

Mrs Fleming had good days and bad. On the good she would sit in a deckchair and read books on the Russian Revolution while insects crawled over her. On the bad she would march round the garden with her buttons in the wrong buttonholes, carrying a portable radio turned up full blast, and shouting at magpies. Her temper changed like the spring skies. She was overjoyed with me when I discovered a pond in one of the dense regions of the bottom bed. 'I'd forgotten all about that,' she said, and she cracked a smile as some lost memory catapulted back. But then she was furious with me when her keys disappeared and she decided it was my fault. 'I open the back door for you and this is what happens,' she raged. My morning was spent searching for them. Eventually they turned up in an empty box of cat food by the dustbin. 'How odd,' she said. 'I don't have a cat.'

I worried about her sometimes, like the day she hung newspapers on the washing line. I said to her, 'Do you have any family, Mrs Fleming, anyone to look after you?' And she replied, 'Harold Pinter of course.'

After a week of land reclaim her garden had become bigger and brighter. I discovered a sundial. I unearthed a path that wound round the outside of the beds and had remained under leaf mould for years. It was enjoyable work, but one garden wouldn't provide me with a living, and despite placing more cards in more shops and even an ad in a local free paper, Mrs Fleming remained my only client. It looked as if I would have to go back to the driving agency, but then I had a call from Miss Clara, and suddenly I was gardener to the stars.

She called one evening when I was sick of answering the phone. This was Neil's fault. He wasn't an easy person to share a flat with. He was probably the only man working in the London property market who was also a disciple of the philosopher Gurdjieff. He spent half his time trying to talk people into investing in endowments, and the other half in search of inner peace and enlightenment which he achieved by attending seminars in Croydon, by putting up posters of Terence Stamp – the star of the newly released biographical film of Gurdjieff – and by placing little cards with aphorisms written on them around the place. I'd look in the sugar bowl and find a card saying: Life is not real until I am.

But these were mildly bizarre traits, all part of sharing a flat, and I would have found them perfectly easy to cope with had it not been for one other part of Neil's make-up which made living with him hell. The awful truth was, he was irresistible to women.

I couldn't understand it. No-one could. He wasn't wealthy, he wasn't a snappy dresser, he certainly wasn't handsome or charming. He was more weird than he was wonderful. And yet women were forever phoning him, knocking on the door for him, sitting next to him on the couch asking him to explain what unit trusts were.

I asked him what his secret was, and he said, 'I've got something every girl is impressed by.'

'What?' – although I wasn't sure I wanted to know.

His piggy eyes quivered. 'An excellent pension.'

Neil had got in on the property market early. He sensed it was about to boom. He'd got himself a mortgage and a pension scheme. He reckoned he was set.

I laughed. 'I don't believe girls are impressed by the size of your pension.'

'Have you got a pension?'

'You know I haven't got a pension.'

'And have you got a girlfriend?'

He knew I hadn't got a girlfriend either. He was just rubbing it in. More likely he was trying to sell me a financial package.

'No I haven't got a girlfriend.'

'See!'

I hadn't got a girlfriend because he had them all. That night a string of women had phoned for him, wanting to know where he was, what time he'd be back, what did he want for his birthday. I let this latest call ring and ring, until I finally grabbed the receiver and said, 'If you want Neil he's out at a Transcendental Meditation seminar with a five foot six blonde called Monica.'

A pause and then a Spanish voice said, 'This is Miss Clara.'

'What?'

'I'd like to speak to the gardener.'

'. . . I'll just get him.'

Miss Clara said she was a housekeeper, but she sounded more important than that. She said she wanted help and she wanted it right away. So the following morning I cycled up the Hampstead hills again, stopping only once to purchase a shiny new trowel. A gardener with his own trowel would, I imagined, make more of an impression. I scuffed it up a bit to age it and then presented myself at some wrought-iron gates on Chesterford Gardens.

It was a fine house, a Georgian facade with a crescent, gravel drive. The heavy gates were locked, but there was an intercom. I pressed the button and before I could say, 'It's the gardener,' the gate buzzed.

Miss Clara opened the front door to me. She had thick black eyebrows and when she smiled she displayed a row of teeth capped with gold that made her mouth glitter. She beckoned me through the house, through large rooms where all the furniture was covered in dust sheets. In the living room a man in overalls polished a wooden floor. In the kitchen a decorator was up a ladder painting the ceiling. The house was being prepared for something.

The back garden was compact and neatly walled, and

compared to Mrs Fleming's was a showcase. It was in need of a spring clean, that was all. There was an overgrown lawn, the beds were littered with last year's debris, and daffodils hung their heads along the borders.

Clara said, 'We want it tidy. Bright and tidy.'

It wouldn't take much, a bit of mowing, bit of weeding, bit of sweeping under the carpet.

'It must be ready in three days,' she added.

I had never thought gardening would involve deadlines, but three days seemed fair enough. 'Fine,' I said, and drew my trowel from my pocket with a flourish to show her I meant business.

There was no need for my own tools, however. When Clara unlocked the garden shed I was presented with a range of quality equipment, barely used. There was a large cardboard box with a picture of an electric mower on it. 'It's new, from Selfridges,' she said. 'You happy?'

'Very happy.'

I set to work. There was a point when I wondered if I would need all three days to assemble the mower, but the morning soon settled down into a familiar session of cutting back and digging up. And every so often Miss Clara would call, 'You want coffee?' and she'd come out with a mug and a nod of approval.

Throughout the day sounds of saws and drills came from inside the house. I saw curtains being put up, then heard someone tuning the piano. I began to wonder who lived there. The house was, if anything, grander from the back than the front, with big bay windows and balconies to the bedrooms. 'Is this your house?' I asked Clara, and she glanced at me severely, but then giggled and focused on a space six inches to the left of my face, the space she always looked at when she talked to me.

'The owner's away, is he?' I asked. But she shook her head, and hurried back into the house.

The owner may have been away, but judging by the preparations – by the army of staff cleaning the place from top to bottom – the owner was coming home.

I had my lunch in the kitchen with the decorator, Pete. When I asked him who lived here he didn't seem to care. He said, 'Some film star, or one of them rock singers.'

'What makes you say that?'

'All the houses are like that up here. You pop in the dry cleaners on Hampstead High Street and there's one of the Bee Gees collecting his shirts. I saw a newsreader jogging across the Heath once.' Pete took a mouthful of his sandwich and spoke so that I could see the pickle. 'I painted the guy-who-lives-next-door-to-Sting's gate. Over in Highgate. Have a look next time.'

That evening I told Neil about the house. He said, 'The Church of Inner Enlightenment have a base around Chesterford Gardens.' He'd been soaking himself in a turmeric-powder bath again and he was a curious shade of yellow. There was a spiritual reason for this ablution but I was never sure exactly what, all I knew was the next person in the bath came out looking jaundiced; you needed another bath afterwards. Now he lay on the floor munching an apple and reading *Life Assurance Monthly*. He looked up with excitement. 'You could be gardening for a maharaja!'

Everyone seemed to have a view on whose house it was. When I told Dick he was intrigued. He quizzed me for clues.

'Any sign of kids?'

'No.'

'Any pets?'

'No. There's a piano.'

'Could be Andrew Lloyd Webber's!'

'And very exotic curtains.'

'Henry Kissinger. He always seems like an exotic-curtain man.'

'Henry Kissinger doesn't live in Hampstead.'

'He lives all over the place.'

'It's not a politician's sort of house.'

'I know! Rod Stewart!'

For the next two days I worked my way systematically through the unknown celebrity's garden, redefining borders, disposing of rubbish in black plastic bags. Meanwhile the house was becoming a home. Window cleaners went through. A security firm serviced the burglar alarm. Rugs were laid. Pete the decorator was sent outside to touch up any paintwork. One afternoon when it started to rain Miss Clara told me I could come into the kitchen to shelter. She was making the room look lived-in, putting groceries in the fridge, pictures on the wall. I said to her, 'How long have you worked here?'

'One year, since they came.'

'Since who came?'

She smiled at me with sealed lips. 'They are coming home soon.'

'Who?'

'The people who live here.'

'It's not Henry Kissinger, is it?'

She appeared timid, but Miss Clara was in charge. She wasn't to be pushed around by anyone. The sound of breaking glass made her hurry up the stairs and then I heard her shouting at a cleaner. While she was out of the room I saw a box on the counter containing photographs in frames. I gently picked one out and saw a picture of a woman, standing at the wheel of a yacht, blown blonde hair, wide mouth, good teeth – American teeth, teeth that looked familiar . . . but I couldn't think from where.

'Farrah Fawcett,' said Dick.

We were trying to write a sketch about a man who had superhuman but useless powers, a man who was able, for example, to go into someone's house and know instinctively where their lost dustpan and brush was. He was known as Dustpan and Brush Man. He dreamed of adapting his skills to do something useful for developing nations.

'It wasn't Farrah Fawcett,' I assured him.

Dick was unable to concentrate. The mystery woman in the photograph had become too much of a distraction. He stared at the ceiling, thinking of blonde women on yachts. 'The blonde one from Abba, Agnatha or whatever her name is.'

'No.'

'Bo Derek.'

'No!'

By Friday the house was ready. Final touches were being applied. Pete the decorator was painting the outside railings. 'I should have been a plumber,' he said, 'they command respect. You don't tell a plumber what to do. He tells you what needs doing.'

Then in the afternoon Miss Clara called to me, 'The flowers are here.'

In the driveway a van from a nursery had pulled up and the driver was bringing out trays of plants. He hung some flowering baskets around the front door and then I helped him carry boxes of bedding plants round into the back garden. They were already blooming. It was simply a case of tucking them into the ground. He took one look at me and said, 'These are alyssum.'

'I know,' I lied.

'And these are petunias.'

'Of course they're petunias.'

'You plant them four to six inches apart, three inches deep, water them well.'

'I know.'

For the rest of the day I dressed the borders. The drabness of the garden disappeared. It was as if I'd coloured it in. It looked like spring had been plugged in and switched on.

And then tables and chairs were put out on the patio. 'What's going on?' I asked Miss Clara.

'It will be a nice evening. We'll have the party in the garden.'

Before I left she handed me my wages in full. 'Pay me in the morning if you like,' I said; 'I'll come round.' I didn't want to leave without solving this. 'I can come on a regular basis if you like,' I said, 'how about that?'

But she was paying me off. 'Just tell me,' I asked her on the doorstep, 'who lives here?'

'No no,' she said and gave me her official shake of the head.

'It is Rod Stewart, isn't it?' But there was a note of panic in my voice. It was too late.

Mandy from downstairs was very disappointed.

'What do you care whose house it was?' I said.

'I sort of had this fantasy it was Meryl Streep's, and you brought her back here for one of your macaroni cheeses, and she needed her hair done.'

'I wouldn't bring Meryl Streep back here.'

'Why not?'

'Neil would get off with her.'

Dick was outraged, so were the staff in the pub where he worked. They had opened a book on the outcome: bets ranged from Sophia Loren to the exiled King of Greece. There was too much money at stake for me not to find out. I was made to promise I would go back the next day and settle the matter.

The next day was Tuesday and I worked at Mrs Fleming's in the morning. She came out with a bucket and collected all the snails she could find. She said she was going to paint them, and I thought she meant a watercolour or something – *Snails in a Bucket*. But she meant paint them all red, so they could be easily found again. I left her watching a TV programme about the rise and fall of the Incas, and I cycled back up to Chesterford Gardens.

Miss Clara seemed to take a while to recognise me. She looked tired. She had her sleeves rolled up and yellow rubber gloves on.

'I left my trowel in the shed,' I lied.

She said nothing, just led me round the side of the house where some men were stacking crates of empty bottles against the wall.

'Some party,' I said. She mumbled some reply. Maybe she was hung-over.

The guests must have spilled out into the garden. I found a champagne cork and a squashed prawn on the lawn. One of the beds had been crushed as if someone had fallen into it. When I went to the shed I found a cigar stub on the window sill.

'You want coffee?' said Miss Clara.

This was what I had hoped, to be asked into the house again. The famous actor/singer/statesman/royal-in-exile would be up by now, walking round in a dressing gown, speaking to their management.

I stepped into the kitchen. It seemed just as many people were at work as before, but this time they were clearing

19

up, putting things away in boxes. And then when I looked into the hallway I could see dust sheets going back over the furniture. The rugs had already been rolled up, the pictures taken down.

'What's happening?' I said. 'I thought they were coming home?'

'They did come home . . .' said Clara, 'and now they are gone again.'

That evening Dick and I finished the Dustpan and Brush Man sketch, but we weren't happy. We hadn't nailed it and we knew it.

We sat in silence. Dick browsed through a copy of the *Standard*. 'Of course!' he said and closed the paper. 'Of course!'

'What?'

'Kathleen Turner. Says here she flew into London yesterday, en route to filming in Egypt.'

'It wasn't Kathleen Turner in the photo.'

'Says here she's an Anglophile.'

'So?'

'So she must have a house in London.'

I looked at her picture in the paper. 'I don't think it was her anyway.'

'But you're not one hundred per cent sure?'

'No.'

'There you go.'

We both thought about Kathleen Turner quietly for a moment, until Dick said, 'It's going to sound very good when we're on chat shows, that is.'

'What is?'

'You used to be Kathleen Turner's gardener.'

I used to be Kathleen Turner's gardener. It did sound good.

3

MRS LAVENHAM

A warm spell and a thunderstorm, that was all it took, and plant life all over London sprouted. Weeds appeared everywhere from Kew Gardens to the cracks in the Kilburn pavements. Homeowners pulled open their curtains and saw their lawns suddenly needed attention. They hunted around for that number of the gardener they had written down weeks ago, and the phone in our house began to ring for me instead of Neil.

A Major Chesney called and asked me to visit him in his house near the Royal Free Hospital. He didn't bother to take me out into the garden. He just stood at his study window and waved his stick in the general direction of the lawn, saying he wanted someone to 'keep it up to scratch'. He had recently lost his wife. Now it was just him and his slobbering old golden Labrador, Carsons. I made a fuss of the dog and easily got the job.

Major Chesney put me in touch with Mr Nugent, who asked me to come and help him tidy his garden because he was selling his house. On my first visit he brought round some prospective buyers as I was clipping the hedge. 'The gardener is included in the purchase price, of course,' Nugent said to them. 'Ha ha!' They didn't make an offer.

Then a woman across the street from Nugent saw me leave and called out from a window. She introduced herself as Annie Kendal. She had a toddler running round her ankles and she was heavily pregnant with her second child. Her husband worked all hours, she said; the garden was too much for them, she said; and they were just recovering from their loft being converted for heaven's sake; so would I mind? She sounded embarrassed to be employing a gardener at all. 'I just want it nice for the summer, for the children, nice and safe, nothing sharp, no ants or anything.'

Word of mouth was doing the trick as I had hoped it would. My calendar started to fill up. There was work here for the whole summer if I could just make it through these opening weeks. 'Gardeners are like gold dust,' one woman said to me, which made me feel wanted, and I thought that as long as I kept to mowing lawns, to raking leaves and killing ants; as long as I didn't try grafting fruit trees or anything flashy; as long as I wiped my feet if I came in the house and inspired some trust, then I could get away with it.

But then Major Chesney sent me round to see an acquaintance. 'Name's Mrs Dunnet,' he said. 'You can't miss her. Sort of blue hair.' It was Mrs Dunnet's house which was more immediately impressive, though. The woman lived behind bars. Each window was protected by a rack of railings. There was a shiny red alarm on the front wall and stickers in the window listing the range of people who weren't welcome, from hawkers to carol singers. She did indeed have blue hair and she had blue fingernails as well, and her garden was as manicured as she was. It looked as though it needed a weekly going-over with a vacuum cleaner rather than a spade and fork, but she told me she required someone to come on a Wednesday morning to mow the lawns because her friends came round in the afternoon to play bridge. 'Visitors do like a nice lawn to look at, I always think.'

I told her I was her man, but then she said, 'I'll need references of course.'

'References!'

'References.'

'What about Major Chesney?'

'I require at least two. Insurance purposes.'

The very word reference brought a smile of submission out of me. I went away mumbling that I would return with the necessary paperwork, but I knew then that if I was serious about this job I would need to become more skilled. I had borrowed gardening books from the library; I'd read gardening newspaper columns and started to take an interest in gardening TV shows, but these were no substitute for the real thing.

What I needed was a teacher. What I needed was Mrs Lavenham.

She lived on a steep hill in Highgate, in a large tree-lined estate, purpose-built in the 1930s. Family houses for the ever-expanding city, with good-sized gardens for professional people who had no spare time and so had to employ gardeners. It was a chain that was profitable for all concerned.

Mrs Lavenham phoned me one evening and said in her BBC voice that she was behind and needed some extra hands. Just the name Lavenham sounded like a flower and made me want to work for her. And then, when I called round, she answered the door wearing cut-off wellingtons and a battered waxed jacket with an RSPB badge on her lapel. In her hand she clutched a pair of secateurs, in her hair was caught what looked like a piece of leaf mould, and I knew I had found my mentor.

She was a keen and knowledgeable gardener, a hardy perennial herself, but arthritis had fastened her joints. She was only in her late fifties I guessed, but if she bent for any length of time she struggled to get up. Her fingers were swollen at the knuckles; her hips creaked. My role was to be her limbs.

Her garden was mature and voluptuous. A honeysuckle had grown so thick and strong it made the arch it climbed over bow in the middle. Ivy crept lovingly over a stone bench. One section of the lawn had been left to produce a meadow. A fig tree spread itself lazily across a sunny wall. It all looked so natural, but it was clear she had worked hard over time to achieve this effect. This winter, however, she'd not been well, she'd let things slip. She said, 'I've never pruned this late before, but I think we'll be all right.'

We started with the roses. And she had roses all over: ramblers spreading over the garage wall, standards posing in the front, miniatures hiding behind drainpipes. She had them in beds, in pots, and twisted into arches. They seemed so precious to her I decided I really ought to come clean and admit my inexperience, but I suspected she knew this already. She smiled knowingly as I pulled out my new gloves. She looked over her glasses at me and said, 'I'll show you how I like them, shall I?'

'Good idea.'

Each rose looked naked as a sheared sheep when she had finished with it, but Mrs Lavenham worked with a cruel-to-be-kind hand. She did three or four and then gave the secateurs to me. 'You have a go.' She sat down stiffly in her foldaway seat and watched as I did the next one, and the one after that and on down the line. 'Those are floribundas,' she said, 'but you probably know that.'

We worked on roses all morning, until at midday she went inside and reappeared with a tray of bread and bits of cheese. Ah, lunch! I thought. But she broke the food up and spread it all over the bird table and along the patio wall. And from all directions the local wildlife appeared: birds, squirrels, the neighbours' cat, a pigeon I was sure I recognised from the Edgware Road, any passing creature got a good feed.

'A garden needs animals,' said Mrs Lavenham.

From roses we moved on to the shrubs, pruning them, feeding them, replanting them. Then at the end of the day we had a big bonfire. Mrs Lavenham was sore but happy. 'Can you come again tomorrow?' she asked. 'We'll tackle the borders. And the lawn needs looking at. It's fun, isn't it?'

That evening I had rose debris in my hair. I had thorns that had pierced my gloves embedded in my hands. I had scratch marks all over my arms. When Dick came round I said, 'Do I smell of roses?'

'No.'

When we started work I told him, 'I feel the need to write a sketch about someone who buys a dozen roses.'

'A time traveller?'

'Why do all your ideas feature time travellers?'

'Why do all your ideas feature flowers?'

'They're funny.'

'Flowers aren't funny.'

'Flowers can be funny.'

'Trust me, flowers aren't funny. Flowers are straight men.'

'Some flowers are straight men, I agree. But some flowers are funny.'

'Name one.'

'Tulips.'

'Not in the slightest bit funny.'

'Snapdragons.'

'Heard them before.'

'All right, red-hot pokers.'

'Red-hot what?'

'Pokers. They're big things on a stem three foot high with a red and yellow bulb on the top, like a clown's nose.'

'You're kidding.'

I showed him a picture of one. He couldn't stop laughing. We wrote a sketch about a branch of Interflora which could send flowers through history: 'A dozen red-hot pokers to Joan of Arc please.' We were heading for the big time, there was no question.

I made sure I kept my regular clients happy. I continued to visit Mrs Fleming and unearth bits of her garden she didn't know she had, and I worked regularly at Annie Kendal's two hours a week, pulling up nettles and making sure the weed-killer stayed on the top shelf, while she sat with her legs in the air and the phone on a long lead by her side. The poor woman was so pregnant she'd lost her patience. I asked her when the baby was due.

'Eleven thirty,' she said without opening her eyes.

I had this image of the ambulance not being able to get through the traffic, of me having to cut the umbilical cord with a pair of shears.

'Shame,' I said. 'I have to go at eleven o'clock.'

I congratulated Mr Nugent on the sale of his house for a

ridiculous sum, and told him I'd happily help him move when the time came. And I'd made a hit with Major Chesney simply by being a friend for Carsons. One pat on the back and the animal followed me round the garden all morning, which was a nuisance, but the major was so pleased the dog had some company. 'He misses you-know-who,' he mumbled.

But it was Mrs Lavenham who saw the most of me. A session with her was like a gardening masterclass. I felt I should be paying her. We tackled the lawn: scarified it, fertilised it, treated it with moss killer, seeded the bald patches. We planted gladioli and dahlia tubers. She introduced me to buddleia and forsythia. If it rained we went into the greenhouse and planted tomatoes.

Her arthritis was affected badly by the weather. When it was wet or the air was damp she seemed to seize up and she winced with the pain. She was a tall woman, but on those bad days she appeared much smaller. She would sit in her chair clutching her tablets and call out instructions to me. I was pruning her apple tree and she said, 'It should be cut back so that a songbird is able to fly through the branches.'

We turned our attention to the borders, cutting back perennials and separating them. 'Would you like some of these?' she'd say, offering me a clump of roots. 'They're Japanese anemone, a pretty pale purple flower in August.'

She wrapped them up in damp newspaper for me. I hadn't the heart to tell her I didn't have a garden. It didn't seem professional for a gardener not to have a garden. I went home and gave them to Mandy downstairs, who had the garden flat. She was very suspicious. 'They're not stolen?'

'No.'

'Not poisonous or nothing?'

27

'They're Japanese anemone.'

'It's drugs, isn't it.'

Mrs Lavenham asked me nothing about my life and rarely spoke of her own. She mentioned a husband once, but as if he was dead. 'He always used to garden in his pyjamas,' she said. 'I never understood why.'

I assumed she lived on her own. Once, when I cut my finger, she took me into the house and got some ice to stop the bleeding and I noticed the freezer was full of little boxes of individual cod portions.

But then one day an upstairs window opened and a thirty-year-old man stuck his head out. He was pale and lean, dressed in a pullover in spite of the warm day. 'We've run out of Lea and Perrins,' he called down. 'Shall I get some from the shop?'

'That's very kind of you, dear,' replied Mrs Lavenham, and the window closed.

She seemed a little embarrassed. 'Have you met Edward?' she asked. 'My son.'

'No.'

She felt she needed to explain. 'He's writing a book . . . on Pope Pius XII.'

'Really.'

'He's written six books, each one on a different pope.'

I couldn't think of any sensible response. 'He's cornered the market, has he?'

'Oh, he's never had one published. We're rather hoping Pius will be the breakthrough.'

She didn't look confident though, as if she knew that Pius was as much of a dud as all the others. I think she disapproved of what Edward did. She hoped it was just a phase. Why couldn't he have been a cardiologist or something normal?

Thanks to this period of intensive training, my confidence rose immeasurably. As we fertilised and mulched, as we went from rockery to soft-fruit patch to lily pond, my knowledge grew and my hands hardened, so that after only a couple of weeks of working for Mrs Lavenham I felt ready to ask her what I hadn't dared ask anyone else: could I have a reference?

She said nothing, just smiled thinly. I wondered if she'd heard and was ignoring me, but as I was about to leave she handed me a sealed envelope with *To whom it may concern* on the front in a flowery hand.

The next day I cycled round to Mrs Dunnet's house. I had no idea what the letter said. 'This man is a reliable employee, a sound gardener and a first-class human being. I cannot recommend him highly enough.' Or: 'Don't let this maniac near your garden; call the police now!'

I rang Mrs Dunnet's bell. The usual number of bolts were withdrawn. But this time she didn't lift off the chain. From behind the door she said, 'Who is it?'

'It's me. The gardener.'

She peered through the gap. I waved the envelope. 'I've got a reference for you.'

I handed her the letter through the crack. She tore it open, read it, then said, 'You're too late. I'm being done by Powerflowers.'

I had thought something looked different. The front garden seemed to have been trimmed to a uniform height. It looked like a team of hairdressers had gone over the place.

'Who are Powerflowers?'

'They've got a white van. They have references and credentials. And nametags.'

And with that she closed the door. 'What about my letter?' I called, but she was already sliding across the deadbolt.

Powerflowers turned out to be a contract gardening company. They did indeed have nametags, and they wore shirts the same colour as the lawn, and they marched in with bags of bark chips and power tools, gave your garden a service and then sent you an invoice with VAT. They were the corporate face of gardening. They wanted to turn every plot into a photograph for their brochure. I regarded them as my enemy, devious and deadly, and over that summer I would come to hate them and everything they stood for, and it wasn't just because the first time I met them they tried to run me over.

4

THE NUGENTS

Neil sat in front of a glass of pale yellow liquid, steeling himself.

'You don't have to do this, you know,' I said to him.

'Yes I do.'

'No, you don't.'

'Everyone in the group is doing it. Drinking your own urine is the purest form of inner cleansing.'

I wished he'd stop calling it his 'own urine', as if on another day he might drink someone else's.

'What sort of religion is it that encourages you to drink your own urine?'

'This isn't a religion. It's a guide for spiritual well-being.'

'Whatever.'

'And if drinking your first urine of the day is what's required I'm not pulling out.'

I wished he'd stop calling it his 'first' urine of the day, as well. This was all before breakfast; this was more than any flatmate should have to endure. And yet I was secretly intrigued, intrigued to see if he would actually go through with it, or whether he was all talk as I suspected.

I said, 'Listen, pretend I'm going to buy a mortgage. And I have a choice of two brokers, and I *just* can't decide which one. Do I go for the broker whose breath smells of the Polo he has just been sucking, or do I choose the broker whose breath smells of . . .'

The phone rang. It was a woman for Neil. 'He's kind of busy at the moment,' I told her.

'Just tell him I've decided not to go to work today. Tell him to call round.'

If Neil managed to maintain his success rate with women after drinking his first urine of the day, then I would start drinking the stuff – mine, that is, not his.

When I got back to him the glass was empty. 'What happened?'

'I did it.'

'No you didn't.'

'I bloody did.'

'You poured it down the toilet.'

'I did not!'

'You liar!'

I was probably reacting more than I would normally have done to one of Neil's fads. But this was because other people's urine was beginning to feature in my life, on a scale I would never have predicted. In the weird and wonderful land of Neil and Gurdjieff it was just about acceptable, but when it surfaced in the genteel world of gardening, well, I was shocked.

It was May by now, and it seemed to me that gardening was the perfect job. I was working outside. I was my own boss and could choose my own hours. I lived in London but went to work in wellies. My commute was a cycle ride across Hampstead Heath.

And gardens were a continual surprise to me. The smell of freshly cut spring grass was intoxicating. And what about laburnum trees? Perfectly normal-looking things until spring, when they suddenly flowered with bright yellow blossoms that hung exotically on the ends of their branches like lanterns. They looked so un-English; they were such a splash and yet somehow I'd managed never to notice them before. The same went for ceanothus with their rich blue pompoms, and as for fuchsia with their flowers that looked like a troupe of scarlet ballerinas, well, they were straight out of some drug-induced dream.

What gardening meant more than anything though, was that I could establish a writing routine. I could garden in the mornings and then meet up with Dick in the afternoons. As the weather warmed we started to meet outside in venues all over London: cafes, parks, museums. All we needed was a pen and a pad and we were away.

Our Interflora sketch was rejected. 'Our trouble is we're ahead of our time,' said Dick. We sat in the Black Lion in West Hampstead and made a pact. We would give it six months. If we hadn't sold a sketch by then we'd pack up.

'Make it eight,' I said.

'All right, eight,' agreed Dick.

'In fact, make it nine. Nine's a good number.'

'Why's nine better than eight?'

'It's rounder.'

'Why not ten then?'

'Ten's not round.'

'Bloody well is.'

'Ten's sort of square.'

'All right! Nine!'

It was all about teamwork.

Annie Kendal had her baby, a little girl. She said she went into hospital at nine o'clock in the morning and came home at five thirty. The miracle of birth had felt strangely like a day at the office.

And there it was, this pink, wrinkly human thing, lying in a pram in the garden. I worked around it as quietly as I could, made sure the shed door didn't bang or the fork tines chink too loudly on stones.

'What's her name?' I asked Annie.

'We . . . don't know,' she said, as if the infant had arrived without a label. 'We can't think of one.'

She couldn't think of a suitable one was what she meant, of course. She looked worried. The baby was two weeks old and they weren't even close to a decision. They'd called her Carolyn for the first forty-eight hours, but then decided against it. 'We thought she was a Carolyn,' sighed Annie, 'but . . . she wasn't.'

They had toyed with Carol, debated Christine, come very close to calling her Camilla. They were stuck in the Cs.

They'd bought name books and made lists. They'd thought about calling her after someone they both admired, but the only person they could agree on was Tony Benn. 'We've only got nine weeks left before we have to register her,' said Annie, as if she saw no solution. Once she pushed the pram over to me as I worked, and sort of hovered.

'Just digging up the brambles,' I said.

She nodded and stood there chewing her lip, then said, 'What do you think?' and she sort of pointed the baby at me.

'About what?'

'What we should call her?'

I liked this; it made me feel useful. I might not have been able to advise this woman on when to prune her wisteria, but I could help in naming her baby.

I looked closely at the blob, the blue eyes, the perfect fingernails, the chubby neck. She looked like a puppy.

'Charlotte!'

'Charlotte?'

'No doubt about it.'

Mrs Kendal pulled a face. 'Charlottes are so . . . bookish.'

'All right. How about calling her after a flower?'

'Like what?'

'Poppy?'

'No.'

'Rose?'

'Never.'

'Lily.'

'No.'

'Iris.'

'Don't be ridiculous.'

'Rosemary.'

'That's a herb.'

Nugent phoned to tell me his house sale had been completed, and they were moving the following week. 'Removals are coming on Thursday,' he told me. 'I'd like some help if you're keen.'

I knew what sort of help he meant. When I had worked there before I had watched him tagging plants, and now he wanted me to dig them up so they could be taken to his new house. He wanted to put the garden in the back of the removal truck.

I called on him the day before the move, and there he was with his wife, emptying the sheds and lining everything up with the pot plants on the patio. He said, 'I've been meaning to ask you. I'll need some help in my new house, you can come along regularly if you like.'

'Fine.'

'Better call me Jeremy.'

'Fine.'

This was a different man to the hard-nosed bargainer I'd worked for before. He appeared uneasy; he was trying to concentrate on the job, on the plants, but I would catch him standing in the middle of the lawn looking wistful, trying to remember what he was meant to be doing. 'I suppose we'll take some montbretia,' he said to me. 'What do you think?'

'Good idea,' and I dug a clump up and put it in a bucket.

Maybe he was just sad to be leaving the house. 'How long have you lived here?' I asked.

'Oh, twenty-five years. Kids were born here.' He smiled at the memory. 'It's been the family home.' He looked tired, as if he was leaving unfinished business.

He sorted through his gardening tools, tried to discuss them with his wife. It was the first time I'd met her and I was hit by the wave of perfume that announced her. You could smell her coming round a corner. She wore big, round sunglasses and had bracelets piled up on her wrists. And she strode about in a businesslike manner compared to her husband's daydreamy amble. There was an air of detachment around her, as if she wanted to get this over and done with. I saw him offer her a stack of pots, and ask her whether she wanted to keep them or not. She waved him away. 'I don't care, I really don't.'

'How about these Japanese anemone?' I asked Jeremy, recognising them from Mrs Lavenham's garden. He nodded and I sliced the spade in and put another clump in a plastic bowl.

I dug up all the herbs from the herb garden. I dug up squares of what he had labelled hypericum. 'Good ground cover,' he said.

I dug up asters and lupins. I dug up phlox, while he stood on the patio staring at the ground. I wasn't sure if he was considering digging up the paving slabs or whether he was just lost in his nostalgia. He picked up a stone hedgehog, studied it and then wrapped it up in newspaper. When he caught me watching him he clapped his hands and said, 'Right! Just about done. One last job.' He led me across the lawn, behind a screen of conifers, to a bottom corner of the garden where there was a small shed, and next to it what appeared to me to be several piles of muddy debris. To Jeremy, however, they were much more than that. He stood over them proudly, paternally even. 'We need to pile these into the trailer,' he said.

'What?'

'These. My compost heaps.'

He was serious. In fact, he was licking his lips at the prospect.

'You're taking your compost with you?'

'Of course I am.' He looked appalled at the very idea of doing otherwise. He was going to fill the trailer and tow it with his car behind the removal van. I thought: 'He's paying me £1.50 an hour; I'll move his compost if he wants me to.'

So we set to work, removing each of the piles shovel by shovel. 'They're different ages,' explained Jeremy, talking about the stuff as if it was Scotch. 'That one is a five-year-old, that's a three, this is six months.' He smelt a handful: 'Long way to go.'

The morning became a voyage into the process of decomposition as I shovelled my way through strata held together with grass cuttings and general garden waste, but spiced with fishbones, eggshells, newspaper, banana skins and tea bags. 'My trick is to liquidise nettles in the blender and pour them over,' said Jeremy. 'It's a big help.' He breathed deeply. 'I think I get more fun out of my compost heap than anything else in the garden.' Then, matter-of-factly, he added: 'Some people even urinate on their compost, you know.'

I must have looked at him oddly, because he tried to explain. 'It's an excellent source of nitrogen.' Now he backtracked. 'I mean, I don't . . . but some people do.' Jeremy would probably have been no less weird than Neil as a flatmate.

The deeper we delved into these heaps the more prehistoric the material that emerged. Centipedes that had been born and raised in this dark realm fell out and scurried for cover. Jeremy seemed to know each layer intimately. He picked out some decaying stems. 'Chrysanthemum. We cleared the bed when we put a swing up for the grandchildren.'

The smell grew more rich the deeper we got, from a vague odour of damp and rot on top, to a pong near the bottom that was how I imagined medieval Britain to smell. 'It's like garden history,' said Jeremy, and he was right, this was compost-dating.

We filled the trailer, making sure the separate heaps didn't mix. Jeremy tied a tarpaulin over the lot and we manoeuvred it out of sight behind the garage. 'It's valuable stuff,' he said in a whisper. 'I don't want it stolen.' He was serious. He had visions of burglars breaking in, thieves who knew what they doing, who ignored the silverware and lifted the compost.

After that the move was complete. Jeremy stood in the middle of the lawn with his hands in his pockets. The garden had gaps now, but it was big enough to cope with this sort of raid. 'The new people will fill the holes,' he said. I must have looked unconvinced. 'Oh, they'll be moving their own plants in,' he added. 'You can guarantee that. Everyone does it.' I was amused at the idea of the plants moving house like the humans, moving up the property ladder, some lowly dog rose from Holloway making it all the way up the hill to mingle with the hybrids of Hampstead. I wondered where Jeremy and his plants were off to next.

'Tufnell Park,' he said when I asked.

That was a surprise – they were going down the hill, the stone hedgehog that he had so lovingly wrapped didn't know it but it was moving down the social scale. 'You'll see the house tomorrow,' said Jeremy. 'You are going to help me replant all these, aren't you?'

I agreed to go to the new house the next day, but then, as I was leaving, Jeremy's wife knocked on the window, and beckoned me inside. She met me at the back door. She took her glasses off, checked Jeremy wasn't around, and then said something very strange: 'I want you to help me move as well.'

'I am helping you move. Jeremy has already asked me.'

She sighed. 'He hasn't told you, has he? He won't tell anyone. We're not moving to the same house.'

I always imagined gardening was an activity that bonded a couple. A garden was a project both husband and wife could involve themselves with: 'You do the flowers and I'll do the veg.' It was a place where they could plough in their differences and emerge with something that was sweet-smelling and tasted good. But the Nugents' garden had become blighted. It was the place where they bickered and battled: what to plant where, which colour lavatera to buy, whether to cut the daffodil stalks down or tie them up. Over the years grievances had escalated, until in the end the garden had become a war zone, two territories divided by a minia-ture privet.

I turned up at Jeremy's new house in Tufnell Park as requested. He seemed very pleased to see me. He gave me coffee and biscuits, then made me sit down and asked me how I was. This was very unusual behaviour for him; he was fussing. He'd already unpacked just about everything. There was a pile of empty boxes stacked by the back door. The house looked very neat, and seemed very bare. 'I always wanted to live without clutter,' he said.

The walls were all painted white. The fridge hadn't one magnet on it. When we finished the coffee he put the mugs in the dishwasher, the coffee jar in the cupboard, and the kettle in a bottom drawer, so that the kitchen tops were as clear as runways. I'd never seen anyone do that before.

Finally he wiped down the surfaces and looked around with satisfaction. 'To work,' he said.

The garden by contrast was full of clutter. He seemed to have got custody of all the tools and most of the plants. His plot was much smaller, but Jeremy was intent on cramming everything in, and there were, as he predicted, gaps where the previous owner had lifted plants.

We spent the morning rearranging the beds, correcting mistakes. 'How could anyone plant a berberis here?' he tutted. 'Ridiculous.'

'Absolutely ridiculous.'

And he was appalled at the quality of the soil. 'No wonder the plants look unhappy.'

All that was about to change though, as we dragged in the compost and scattered Jeremy's premium five-year-old all over the beds. He had the look of a Red Cross worker. The plants were the innocent victims of famine and he was the volunteer bringing relief. 'It's shocking!' he announced. 'No worms anywhere. You can tell the quality of the soil by the number of worms. We need to attract worms!'

He was liberal with the compost and ordered me to be the same. He worked with such gusto it was as if this was therapy for him. Compost was a panacea that encouraged rebirth and growth. At the end of the morning we heeled in the plants from the old house. 'I think they'll be happy here,' said Jeremy, and he unwrapped his stone hedgehog and found a place for it on a low wall.

He offered me some soup for lunch. We unfolded his garden furniture and sat on the patio.

'It's smaller but gets better sun. That's why I chose it.' He smiled, smacked his lips. 'I'm very pleased with it.' He was trying to convince himself he was happy. 'My daughter's coming this evening. She only lives in Archway, nice and close.' Then he said, 'What do you do, anyway?'

He was the first person I had gardened for who had asked me this, and the question suddenly made me feel sorry for him. He was trying to make an effort. He was on his own now and he knew he was going to have to be nicer to people. His wife had got custody of their friends. He was going to have to make new ones. He wanted me to be his friend.

'I'm a gardener,' I said.

'No,' he said. 'You know what I mean.'

'Well . . . I'm a writer as well.'

'Ah, I thought so,' he said. 'What do you write? Books?'

'TV. Comedy sketches . . .'

He seemed thrilled. 'Really? For whom?'

I felt myself redden. I knew I was about to lie to him. 'Two Ronnies,' I said.

'Ah. Goodnight from him and goodnight from him.'

'That's them.'

41

'We used to watch them . . . we used to . . .' But he stopped, he was remembering sitting down with his family on Saturday night watching *The Two Ronnies*. 'My wife didn't like them.'

'They're not everyone's cup of tea.'

'No.'

He put his soup bowl down, and looked up at the sky. 'It's going to rain.' Then he asked coyly, 'Do you want to . . . do you want to . . . see the site for my new compost heap?'

'OK.'

'You don't have to.'

'I'd like to.'

'You're sure now?'

'Positive.'

Later in the week I went to Jeremy's wife's new house. She was as friendly to me as he had been. They both wanted to prove to me they weren't the guilty party. 'Did you tell him you were coming here?' she asked, and she looked over my shoulder, as if I might have been followed.

Her house felt crammed compared to his. She'd got all the ornaments and paintings, the silverware, the things. She was still unpacking. She asked me to hold a picture up against the wall and then she stood back to take a look. 'Bit higher, left side up a bit.' She pulled a face. 'No I don't think so.'

The garden was just a big patio, the only earth was in narrow beds round the edges. She'd not taken any of the plants from the old garden and I wondered what she wanted me to do, but then she drove me down to the garden centre and there she bought nothing but climbers: morning glory, clematis, honeysuckle. 'It's the garden I've always wanted,' she said, as we drove back. 'I want these things to creep

round and meet each other and eventually form a shroud.'
She laughed but she sounded scary.

After we'd planted them she gave me tea and asked, 'So what's his garden like?'

'It's . . . nice.'

'I bet.' She rolled her eyes and tried not to be bothered. Then she said, 'I feel like a proper drink. Do you want a drink?'

'No thanks.'

'Go on.'

'All right.'

She poured two gin and tonics, then kicked her shoes off and put her feet up on a stool. The sight of her toes made me want to go home.

'Those beds could use some compost,' I said, trying to make conversation. But of course it was precisely the wrong thing to say. The atmosphere chilled. Ice chinked in the glasses. She looked at me sternly and said, 'Do you know, he used to pee on it.'

I said nothing. I wasn't taking sides.

'He used to save his urine in jars. Then last thing at night he'd go down and pour it all over his compost heaps. Sometimes he used to climb on top of them and pee on them in the moonlight. How strange is that?'

Not that strange, but it was clear that compost had had an unhealthy effect on their marriage; it could even have been the grounds for their separation. She had had enough. She had given him an ultimatum. Jeremy had been forced to choose between his wife and his mouldy mistress, and he had chosen his mistress.

5

LADY BRIGNAL

I went to a party and chatted to a girl who worked for a bank. She asked what I did, and I said, 'I spend half my time gardening and the other half writing comedy.'

'It must be hard to get by.'

'It is.'

'Persevere and you'll get there. I know lots of people who would love to be a gardener.'

The idea that I was writing scripts to keep me going until the day I could become a full-time gardener was one I hadn't considered, and I was going to put her right, but then I realised she would have been disappointed. Gardening had a certain sex appeal, more sex appeal than sitting in a room in Hackney writing unsolicited sketches for *The Two Ronnies* did, anyway. Gardening was earthy. It was the perfect combination of creativity and freedom. It conjured up escape. With spring in the air it was even romantic. Quite how romantic I didn't realise until I went to work for Lady Brignal.

It was Pete the decorator who found me the job. Pete and

I frequently crossed paths now. We both worked the same patches, the same estates. People who employed jobbing gardeners were the same sort of people who employed jobbing decorators.

Pete was well aware of the sexual undertones of gardening. 'I mean the lady of the house is always falling for the gardener, isn't she? It's kind of traditional. Lady Chatterley and all that.' We were sitting on a bench eating lunch at the bottom of Parliament Hill. His hands were splashed with emulsion; mine were matted with mud. 'But no-one ever falls for the decorator,' he grumbled. 'In ten years of this business no-one has ever made a pass at me.'

Pete seemed unhappy in his work. It wasn't that he disliked painting and decorating, he just found it unfulfilling. 'I thought people would want to have their rooms painted aubergine and terracotta,' he confessed to me, dreamily. 'I thought they might even want murals. I thought I might make a difference, you know. But they just shove a tin of Soft Peach at me and say, "Have it done by Thursday."'

We often found jobs for each other. I sent Pete round to Major Chesney's when he was looking for someone to paint his hallway brown. Pete sent me round to a house in Dartmouth Park where the woman wanted her garden 'to look . . . better than next door's'. When Pete decorated a kitchen for a Lady Brignal, and she said she was looking for a gardener, he quickly passed on the information to me.

I wasn't sure I wanted the job at first.

'Why not?' said Pete.

'Those sort of people make me . . . clumsy.'

'What sort of people?'

'Aristocrats. I drop things when I'm in their company. I'm all fingers and thumbs.'

But Pete told me not to worry about Lady Brignal. She

was all right, he said. He had almost convinced her to have her kitchen painted Minoan Red. 'She went for Apple Blush in the end. Looks horrible.'

'Tell you something else,' he said. 'A very handsome woman, is Lady Brignal. Good bones.'

I assumed Lady Brignal's house would be grand, the sort of abode that went with a title, but the address Pete gave me was a regular, terraced property off Rosslyn Hill with hardly any front garden at all. There was no gravel drive, no coat of arms on the gate, no hint of nobility at all. I knocked; a dog barked, and a woman pulled open the door holding back a spaniel. She was in her twenties, dressed in jeans and a T-shirt. She wore no shoes and had her hair tied up loosely so strands fell round her face. She was three steps up from me and I noticed her toenails were sprinkled with glitter.

I wasn't sure if she was Lady Brignal or Lady Brignal's daughter. I said, 'I'm the gardener. Pete the decorator told me . . .'

There was never any question of references. Pete's word was good enough. She ushered me in, gave me coffee, told me to call her Helen, then opened the door to the terrace. She stood with her hands in her back pockets and said almost apologetically, 'This is it.'

The garden was dark and mossy. The only colour was the white blossom of a leggy lilac that was crying for light. The lawn had bare patches; the shrubs overhung and dripped. 'What do you think?' she said.

'It needs . . . to breathe.'

'That's what I think. It's a bit gloomy. All this . . . stuff needs to go,' and she waved her hand at the overgrown shrubs. She was the youngest client I had ever had and the first one to know less about plants than I did.

'I'll cut everything back,' I said. 'Let in the light.' She was looking at me and nodding. I was reassuring her. It felt very good.

'I'll do something with the lawn as well, and put a few hanging baskets about the patio.' I had learnt that if I wanted to swing a job I needed to mention hanging baskets somewhere in my pitch. Hanging baskets were the sort of words clients wanted to hear; they meant colour, they meant summer, they meant sitting outside with a drink, and friends saying, 'Oh, I do like your garden.'

'I'll show you the shed,' said Helen.

The shed was held together with moss. She tugged at the door and the whole thing creaked and swayed. Inside was a collection of gardening equipment from the 1950s. 'Is this OK?' she asked.

I was suddenly conscious of being in a small space with an attractive woman of good breeding. It didn't matter that we were in a musty hut surrounded by rusting gardening tools, in fact that might have added something to the general sensuality. I stole glances at her. I wondered if she was married. Maybe this was the town house, the garret she and the lord kept for overnight visits when they came down from their country seat in Bedfordshire. Or maybe she came here to get away from him. Yes, that was probably it.

'This is fine,' I said.

'Well I'll leave you to it.'

She looked far too pretty in the shed light. I folded my arms self-consciously and knocked a jar of nails off the window sill. The clumsiness had kicked in.

She smiled, a coy smile. 'I'll leave you to it,' she said again.

It wasn't difficult work – a pair of shears, a pruning saw and some secateurs, and more cutting back, more destruction.

But what made this the best job I'd had so far was the music that came from the house all morning. I pruned the forsythia to the beat of Elvis Costello. I deadheaded the daffs to Ian Dury's *New Boots and Panties* — I had that album myself. Helen and I liked the same music; we had a lot in common. Maybe she was divorced, and this house was part of her settlement. Yes, that was probably it.

It didn't take long to let light into the garden. I worked my way through the overgrowth like a musketeer works his way through a gang of desperadoes: with speed and leaving a pile of amputated mess. I glanced up at the house from time to time but there was no sign of her, just the music coming from an upstairs window. She worked her way through a Squeeze album, then an Ultravox, a Joe Jackson. When the end of the session came I didn't want to leave.

Eventually I poked my head indoors and called her name. The music stopped and I heard her pad across the landing. I had time to peek into the living room. I saw a thick white carpet and many paintings, including a large canvas above the mantelpiece that featured peacocks. Helen wasn't married or divorced. She was the daughter of Lord and Lady Brignal and she had been sent up to town to work in an art gallery on Bond Street. Yes, that must have been it.

She came trotting down the stairs, clutching money. When she handed me my £3 the notes were warm.

'That's great,' she said, looking out through the kitchen.

'Next time I'll tackle the lawn. You can sit outside.'

'I'll be lucky,' she said, which sounded sad.

The spaniel came bounding up. I tickled its chin.

'What's its name?'

'Byron,' she said. 'Silly name really.'

And that was when I decided that she was caught here, in this house, in this life, where she had to remember her position, where dogs had to be called after poets, where she was expected to sit inside all the time and study the history of art. She was here against her will, and I needed to rescue her.

The first thing I had to do was win her confidence, show her that it wasn't a sexual thing, that my motive was chivalrous. The best way to do that, I decided, rather oddly, was by making a good job of her garden. During the week I went to the Swiss Cottage library and studied a range of *How to Look after Your Lawn* books. They all wanted me to dig it up, rake it, roll it and resow it. But digging up Lady Brignal's lawn was more than my confidence would allow, so I asked down at the local garden centre. There the manager, a man named Bernie who wore a tie with tulips on it, said, 'You've got to know what you're doing if you want to dig up a lawn.'

I was about to tell him I knew exactly what I was doing, but then I remembered that I didn't.

It occurred to me that a man who ran a garden centre could be useful to me over the coming summer, and so I looked up at him as an apprentice would a master and asked what I should do. He leaned forward and with all his experience and wisdom said, 'If I was you I'd bung some grass seed down and hope for the best.'

Dick was appalled by the ease with which I had become beguiled by Lady Brignal. He said, 'I don't know if I can write comedy with someone who is a servant of some bloated plutocrat.'

'She's not bloated,' I protested. 'She's got good bones.'

'She's got you eating out of her hand.'

'Not true!'

But it was true. I knew because the next time I was due

to work at her house I woke early, bathed and shaved, and put on my Grateful Dead T-shirt.

It was a memorable day, not least because as I cycled to work I had my first encounter with Powerflowers.

They got me with a routine I should have seen coming, the one all cyclists hate, the overtaking-and-then-turning-sharp-left trick, a manoeuvre that leaves you with nowhere to go but up the kerb. I landed with a crash on the pavement. I was lucky – I suffered nothing more than a skinned and bruised arm – but I was also angry. When I saw the van had stopped a little further up the road I had to say something.

There were four of them piling out – one who looked like the foreman and drove the van, and a gang of three to do the spadework. They all had their smart green T-shirts on, but they were an ugly bunch. I marched up to the foreman, whose nametag read Don. 'I guess you didn't see me back there, did you?'

Don looked at me, wondered whether to ignore me, but then said, 'Yeah I saw you, you were on the bike.'

'You knocked me off.'

'No I didn't.'

'You forced me into the kerb. I came off,' and I showed him my bloodied arm.

Don just took his shovel off the back of the van and headed for the house with the rest of the crew.

'You forced me into the kerb,' I said again.

Now he stopped and turned, and took three big steps towards me as if to confront me. He gave me a stubbly grin. 'Listen. Do yourself a favour and get lost. This is a tough business.'

'What is?'

'Gardening.'

I stood there and watched him go into the house. How did he know I was a gardener?

Lady Brignal was very sympathetic. She let me wash my arm in the kitchen sink and then she found some plasters and Germolene. I couldn't see to the wound with one arm, so she dabbed it dry and then smeared the cream on and pressed the plaster onto my skin.

'Powerflowers do some houses on this street,' she said. 'They play Radio One all the time while they work,' and she shook her head in despair.

'That's terrible,' I said. I could smell her hair as she bent to put the plaster on.

'I don't think they're even gardeners,' she said.

'That's outrageous!'

'The manager comes round and does the smooth talking and then the cowboys move in.'

'They said gardening was a tough business.'

'Maybe it wasn't an accident? They probably think you're muscling in on their patch.' She laughed. But I didn't think it was funny.

'I don't want to upset them,' I said. 'They've got chain-saws!'

Patched up, I went into the garden and started work on the lawn. She disappeared upstairs and I waited for the music to start again. She began with the Clash then moved on to the Stranglers and then more Elvis Costello, her favourite. I wondered what she was doing up there – lying on cush-ions, browsing through art catalogues? Or maybe writing letters to multi-conglomerates asking for donations to worthy charities?

Once I looked up and saw her looking back down at me as I scattered grass seed. She gave a little wave. I gave a little wave back. Maybe she was married after all, but she was imprisoned in a marriage. It had been arranged by her evil stepfather. I spent the rest of the morning lost in a fantasy where I met her walking across the Heath one evening and we got talking and got along so well that I suggested we went to the Hollybush Inn. There we sat in one of the booths and she started to tell me what a burden it was having a title and how she didn't really want this life; she was too young to have got married and her husband was away all the time anyway in Argentina where his business interests lay, and all she really wanted to do was go back to her job as a music teacher which was what she'd been doing before she met him and where she had been happiest and . . .

'It's gone twelve o'clock, you know.' It was Helen standing by the back door, telling me I'd gone over.

'Lost track,' I said. 'I was enjoying the music.'

She gave me my money. I said, 'Don't let the dog on the seeded bits for a few days.'

'You hear that, Byron?' She called the dog to her side.

I tickled his chin again. When in doubt pat the dog. Then she said, 'I'm just taking him out onto the Heath.'

Five minutes later I was walking by the ponds with her, pushing my bicycle. She threw a stick along the path for Byron. I said, 'If I had a dog I think I'd call it Elvis.'

We climbed Parliament Hill and gazed down into the hazy city. 'What was the first record you ever bought?' I asked.

'A Billy Fury one. I forget the title.'

'"Fool's Errand?"'

'Can't remember. What was your first?'

'"Singing the Blues" by Tommy Steele.'

She cringed, but she was enjoying herself.

There was a nip in the air and the sky was the colour of concrete. Helen said, 'It's supposed to be spring but it feels like it's going to snow.' I resisted the urge to put my arm round her.

A Tesco plastic bag darted towards us on the breeze and landed at our feet. She picked it up and screwed it into a ball. 'My sister met her husband in Tesco,' she said. 'He took her trolley by mistake. She started shouting at him and afterwards he had the nerve to ask her out.'

Byron had met a retriever and was chasing it across the grass down to the lidos. 'Where's your next job?' she asked.

'Up there,' I said, pointing in the general direction of Highgate.

'You're the gardener to the rich and titled, are you?'

'I suppose so.' I wasn't making good conversation, but I didn't want to know any more details about her, or her sister, or anyone she knew. I didn't want to break the spell. I just wanted her to run away with me, away from this rarefied place, down into the dens of Kilburn. I said, 'Do you want to know my favourite part of the Heath?'

'Where?'

'I'll take you.'

We walked after Byron, through the woods along the edge of Kenwood House, past a vast sweaty jogger who looked as though he needed oxygen, past a woman lying in the middle of the little football pitch doing stretches in an anorak, past a couple sitting on a bench having an argument, until I found what I was looking for, the little rusty bridge that crossed some nameless brook.

'Here, I like this bit the best.'

'It's like lots of other bits.'

'No. This bit's different.'

It was different. It was a lost corner. There was no litter, no sound of traffic, no footprints, no sign of anyone apart from the graffiti scratched on the ironwork. The only reminder of the city was the fat London pigeons that sat in trees bending the branches to breaking point.

We leaned against the bridge railings. Lily pads had covered the stream below so you wouldn't have known there was water there. I edged fractionally closer to Helen's elbow. She closed her eyes and turned her face to the sky. 'When I was a little girl, my father used to bring me to Hampstead. We lived out in Essex, but I always wanted to live here.'

She was an Essex girl who had married for money. I edged another centimetre nearer to her. At this rate I would be touching her by sunset.

I said, 'Your wish came true.'

She looked confused. 'I don't live here.'

I looked at her for an explanation. She had definitely said she didn't live here. Maybe she was implying that although she lived here literally, metaphorically she lived somewhere altogether different.

'What do you mean you don't live here?'

'I live in Finsbury Park.'

I was lost now. 'Why . . . so why are you . . . ?'

'I'm the cleaner. I clean the house. You didn't think . . .'

'No. No . . . of course not.'

'I just clean and take the dog out, go to the shops for them. I do a number of houses, like you do. I'm trying to be an actress. Do you do anything else?'

'Pardon?'

'Do you do something else, apart from gardening?'

'Yes. Writer.'

'Thought so. My boyfriend's a writer.'

I was trying hard not to show what a fool I felt, but I didn't manage it. She started to laugh. 'You really thought I was Lady Brignal, didn't you?'

'No.'

'Yes you did!' and she poked me. 'You thought you were out walking with a Lady, but you got the cleaner instead,' and she laughed and laughed. 'What a disappointment.'

'I'm not disappointed.'

'You look it.'

'I'm glad you're not a Lady, some bloated plutocrat.'

'Lady Brignal's not bloated. She's a handsome woman.'

The cold air had come between us now. We were inching apart. And she was right, of course, I did feel disappointed.

'Are you writing for TV?' she asked.

'Yes.'

'Comedy?'

'Yes.'

'Michael writes drama.'

'Who's Michael?'

'My boyfriend.'

Twenty seconds ago I had been about to take her away from all this. Now I was on first-name terms with her boyfriend.

'What are you acting in?'

'Nothing,' she shrugged. 'I did an advert last year, for digestive biscuits. It's not easy.'

'No.'

'I had a walk-on in an episode of *Doctor Who* once.'

We watched a heron land on a distant tree, like a jump jet on the *Ark Royal*. For some reason I had always thought I was the only struggling artist up here, the only one trying to make a living off the wealthy folk of Hampstead. But the place was probably crawling with would-be writers, actors, musicians, all of us doing service jobs, waiting for a break, for the day we came good and could employ gardeners, decorators and cleaners of our own.

'I've got to get back,' she said. 'Come on, Byron.'

'I'll see you next week,' I called. I didn't want her to go. 'I'll bring some of my records.' I was trying too hard.

She waved without turning round. 'If you want,' and she strolled off, swinging the dog lead. I'd thought she was trapped, but she had an even less stressful life than I did. And as I watched her walk away I realised why I had felt so disappointed that she wasn't Lady Brignal. It was because she didn't need me to rescue her any more. In fact she didn't need me at all.

Having worked this out I began to find her more attractive than ever.

6

MS PEEK AND
MR JACKSON

I decided to adopt a means test the day a client paid me
with a cheque from a bank so posh I'd never heard of it.
From then on I raised my standard charge of £1.50 an hour
to £1.75 if my employer had more than one vehicle in the
drive, or more than one surname, or if they had a view of
the Heath. This allowed me to knock 25 pence off at the
other end of the scale, for an OAP, say, who couldn't really
afford a gardener but had ragwort climbing in through her
bedroom window. It was a small and rather pathetic attempt
at redistributing the enormous wealth of NW3, but
strangely satisfying.

Single mothers qualified for this concession, and this was
the category Ms Joan Peek fell into. She lived in Crouch
End, which was out of my target area, but she said she'd
seen my advert while walking on the Heath, and did I ever
come her way? She sounded forlorn.

Her flat was on the route to Dick's pub so it was no trouble to go round, but this was unlike any other house I'd been asked to. The first time I called on her she answered the door clutching her small child, who was crying his eyes out. Then I noticed she had tears in her own eyes. I had arrived in the middle of a scene, and I wondered whether I should burst into tears myself to show some solidarity.

Joan blew her nose and took me through into the garden, which was basically three beds of monster weeds and a washing line. 'I don't get the time,' she sniffed. 'I don't get any time any more . . .' Her bottom lip began to go again. I took the job just to stop her crying. I felt so sorry for her. She was no older than I was, but her life was so different. She looked as though she'd been abandoned. Hers was no comfortable home with family snaps on the mantelpiece, no shiny new toys or activity frames in the garden. The fridge didn't even have any party invites stuck on it. She had a sliced white loaf and a jar of honey on the table, and she was on her own. To take 25 pence off my hourly rate seemed the least I could do.

How different were the circumstances of the other single parent I worked for, a man named Graham Jackson. His status qualified him for the concessionary rate, but his cream linen suits, and the gleaming soft-top Mercedes parked in the garage of his smart house in Highgate, immediately bumped him up into my super-rate bracket. His three-year-old boy, Frank, probably had more in his Young Saver's Account than Joan Peek did in her whole world. Just looking round the garden it was clear that – a live-in mother aside – here was a household with everything. A trampoline stood on the lawn, a Wendy house under the trees at the bottom, a swing here, a hammock there. Had Frank asked for a roller coaster it would have been up and operational by the weekend.

Graham went off to work all day; Frank went to his Junior Investors Child-care group in the City; and I was left to myself. Their garden was a pleasing walled plot, cottage-style, informal and well-stocked from the garden centre with plants that still had price tags on and, helpfully, instructions on how to look after them. This was a good place to daydream the morning away, and I began to wonder how a situation could be contrived to bring Joan and Graham together. She would get her bills paid, her boy Jamie would get a kid brother he could beat up, and Graham would get . . . Graham would get nothing he wanted or needed.

And maybe that was the real reason I charged Graham more than I charged anyone else. It wasn't because he was wealthy, he was just too damn smug. I suppose he had every reason to be. He was charming, fit, wealthy and good-looking. But he had also a smirk, a smirk that said: you can do what you like, you won't get the better of me. It was a challenge I couldn't resist.

I did the whole of Joan's garden in less than a two-hour session. It was like clear-cutting a miniature forest. Once all the giant weeds were gone, I discovered there was absolutely nothing in the beds apart from one pale rose which now stood cowering, waiting for the chop. When Joan saw the devastation her eyes began to water again.

'Don't worry,' I said. 'We can put plants in.'

'I can't afford plants!' she whimpered.

'Oh, plants are everywhere. I'll get you plants.'

When I got home I asked Mandy from downstairs for a clump of the Japanese anemone back.

'You can have the lot,' she said. 'They don't do anything.'

'I told you they don't flower until August.'

'That's when I go on holiday!'

So I took a clump and replanted them in Joan's bald beds. 'They look lonely,' she said quietly, tearfully.

'They'll spread,' I said. 'I'll get more stuff anyway.'

Again I asked Mandy. This time I was after her Michaelmas daisies.

'Why me?' she moaned. 'You spend all day in rich people's gardens stuffed with flowers but you want to nick mine!'

She was right, of course. Lots of my clients had more plants than they knew what to do with. I could rehouse them at Joan's. It was the natural thing to do, and the most natural client to do it from was Graham Jackson.

The next time I was at his house I came across a mass of yellow things I didn't know the name of but which had spread all across the back wall and were making a bid for the front. They needed to be culled; they needed to be removed. I thought about it all morning – thought about whether I should ask permission, but I liked the idea of using Graham Jackson, and so just before I left I sliced the spade into them, ripped out a bunch by the roots, dunked it in the pond, put it in a plastic bag, strapped it to the back of my bike and crept out of there with my head down.

Twenty minutes later the plant was recovering in Crouch End. It never knew what had happened to it, and neither did Graham Jackson.

That was just the start, of course. From there I progressed to handfuls of forget-me-nots tucked into my coat pocket, then a clump of montbretia stuffed under my pullover. Each time I passed through Crouch End I called in at Joan's and dug in one of Graham's plants. I felt like Robin Hood.

'Where do you get these from?' she asked when I

presented her with a carrier bag of lily of the valley.

'Found them,' I said. 'They're everywhere.'

She laughed as she said, 'All I need now is some nice garden furniture.'

'Mmm,' and I pictured myself strapping Graham's luxury recliner to the back of my bike, hoping he wouldn't miss it. Joan saw me working this through and said, 'Only joking.' Then she brought a kitchen chair out and put her feet up on a stool and did one clue of the crossword, after which little Jamie woke up with a scream.

The truth was I was becoming too ambitious. One morning I found a toy in Graham's bottom bed, a wooden train with two carriages that had been lying there a while by the look of them. Young Frank probably didn't know he'd lost them, so at the end of the session I slipped them into my jacket.

Joan wondered what I was doing when I handed the train to Jamie. 'I was given it,' I said. Jamie clasped it closely and then fell to the ground and started pushing it along, making reassuring chuffing noises. It hadn't been played with in such a way since it came out of its box.

Joan's beds started to fill up. I got some clients to donate plants: Mrs Lavenham happily offered some lupins; Major Chesney gave me some of his London pride for the borders. I even talked Jeremy Nugent into giving me some of his lavender: 'Going to a good home I assume?'

But I always stole from Graham Jackson. Not because I thought he would say no had I asked him, but because I imagined I was putting one over on him. Graham thought he owned everything, but he didn't own me.

Then one morning as he paid me, he gave me his smug smile as usual, but then he winked at me, and in a flash I knew he knew what was going on. Rather than accuse me, however, he was going to make a game of it. He was going to get even with me, and he was going to have fun doing it.

Dick and I had had a small success. A script editor at the BBC had written back telling us that one of the reasons our sketches were being rejected was that they didn't suit any of the shows in development at that time. We needed to find out what programmes had been commissioned, and then write with specific performers in mind.

'Pretty obvious, really,' said Dick.

'Blindingly obvious.'

The script editor then invited us into the Television Centre to have a chat.

'It's our first break,' said Dick, and proposed we take the rest of the afternoon off to celebrate.

'What are you going to wear?' I asked him as we sat in the Black Lion.

'What I always wear, of course. I'm not pandering to the bloody BBC. I've got my integrity to live with . . . why, what are you wearing?'

I had already thought what I would wear for our first ever visit to the BBC: the sky blue jacket I got for my eighteenth birthday.

'You're going to wear that awful old blue jacket, aren't you?' said Dick.

'No, course not.'

The day of our BBC meeting was the day I did Graham's garden. My plan was to work there for a couple of hours, come home, shower and change and meet Dick outside White City station at one thirty. But when I got to Graham's house there was a crisis. Frank's childminder hadn't turned up. Graham had phoned her, but there was no answer. He assumed she was on her way, but he should have left for work himself ten minutes ago, and he was itching to get going. Despite his money Graham's lifestyle wasn't foolproof. Unlike Joan, who was always available and always flexible, Graham depended on a tight schedule and a range of minders to ferry Frank from one activity to the other, and then to take care of him until Daddy got home from his long day. If anything went wrong there was a chain reaction and the whole process collapsed.

'She's probably caught in traffic,' he said. 'Be here any minute.' He delivered this information in a very soft and calculated voice. Other, lesser people would have been panicking by now. Not Graham. He had assumed a Zen-like composure. He seemed calmer in a crisis than out of one. But the clock was ticking. He made calls to work. It was clear he had to get there fast. I sensed that if he didn't make it in by ten o'clock millions would be lost, maybe the whole economy would go under.

He went next door to ask a neighbour, no luck. He phoned his ex-wife, no answer. He turned to me and said in a very relaxed manner, 'I'm going to ask you to do something I wouldn't normally ask a gardener to do . . .'

Two minutes later Frank and I were watching a video while Graham's Mercedes sped him into the City. 'I don't want to watch TV,' announced Frank. As well as his father's confidence and big ears he was gaining his father's smirk.

'What do you want to do then?' I said. I wasn't familiar with the role of childminder, but kids were just kids, I could handle this tyke, just let him know who was in charge.

'Lets play hide and seek,' squealed Frank and he ran out through the French windows and into the garden.

Twenty minutes later the childminder still hadn't turned up, which was a good job because I still hadn't found Frank.

'Come on Frank. Where are you! I mean it!' My voice had gone past the let's-play-along-with-this stage and was climbing the scale towards desperation.

I couldn't have lost him in the garden. I knew the place better than he did. I searched the shed; I searched the shrubs. I called and called his name but the little bugger wasn't coming out. He must have ducked back inside the house when I wasn't looking.

So I went and searched in areas of the house a gardener isn't normally allowed to see. I searched in cupboards; I searched in chests. I went upstairs and looked in the laundry basket. I looked in an ottoman on the landing. I searched in wardrobes and discovered Graham had a very butch kimono with a snake on the back, and more shoes than Freeman Hardy and Willis.

The phone rang and I grabbed it. I had a terrible vision of little Frank calling me from a phone box in Leicester Square.

'It's Graham.'

'Hi Graham.'

'Is Jenny there yet?'

'Not yet.'

'Sorry about this. Everything all right?'

'Fine. Fine.'

'What are you doing?'

'Watching telly.'

'Good. Got to go. She'll be there soon. Huh.'

'Huh.'

I searched in the garage. I searched the garden again. I emptied the shed. I tried to think where I'd hide if I was a kid. Of course! The airing cupboard.

I spent a long time trying to find the airing cupboard. And when I managed it there was no sign of him. Eventually

I heard a laugh from downstairs and found him back in the living room watching TV.

'Where have you been?'

'Watching *Mr Men*.'

I needed to regain control. 'You're not watching TV in the daytime,' and I switched it off. 'We'll read a story.'

I spent the next hour reading him stories from the Mr Men books. Frank liked Mr Noisy, and insisted I shout the lines in character.

'I want two pounds of sausages and . . .'

'Not loud enough,' said Frank.

I raised my voice. 'I want two pounds of sausages and . . . !'

'Still not loud enough,' said Frank.

'Two pounds of sausages and a . . . !'

'Louder,' giggled Frank.

Mr Jelly was a safer bet, but of course Frank wanted me to wobble about when I read it. When he pushed Mr Tickle at me I decided to revise my decree about daytime TV.

By now the Test Match was on. 'Let's watch the cricket,' I said.

'I want *The Wombles*.'

'Cricket!'

'*Wombles!*'

'I'll give you a chocolate biscuit if we watch the cricket.'

'Two chocolate biscuits.'

'It's a deal.'

'And a glass of Daddy's wine.'

'You're not having Daddy's wine.'

'*Wombles*.'

'All right, bloody *Wombles*.'

By eleven thirty the childminder still hadn't shown, and

now it was time for me to get going to the BBC. The phone rang – Graham again.

'She's still not here,' I told him.

'I know, she's just called me. She said her flat caught fire. What time do you have to go?'

'Now.'

'Can you stay a little longer? I'll try and get someone else.'

'I can't, really . . .'

'I'll pay you extra, of course. Overtime. Double. Three pounds an hour.'

Three pounds an hour. The guy had more money than sense. What was I worrying about anyway? I had plenty of time. I'd cycle fast and just have a wash instead of a shower. I agreed to stay until twelve thirty.

At twelve Frank said, 'It's lunchtime.'

'Bit early for lunch.'

'It's lunchtime!'

'All right.'

The fridge was one of those huge American-style things that takes up one side of the kitchen and rumbles like an upset stomach. It was stocked like Harrods Food Halls.

Frank pulled out some Parma ham and smoked salmon.

'That's what you have for lunch?'

'With crisps and Fanta.'

Fine by me.

'Now I want pudding,' said Frank.

'What do you normally have for pudding?'

He thought for a minute. 'I dip my fingers in the chocolate-spread jar.' He was getting the hang of this.

Twelve thirty and I really had to go, but still no sign of a childminder. I called Graham's office. 'He's in conference,' said his secretary. 'He'll be out in half an hour.'

'It's an emergency.'

She made me hold. And it was as I was waiting on the phone that I realised: this was all part of a plan. Graham had known I was stealing his plants from the start, and had been biding his time until he could get revenge. He was waiting until he could hit me where it hurt. Somehow he had discovered about my meeting, and now he was going to derail my career before it had even got moving. Well, I wasn't going to fall for that.

Graham came on the line. 'I've got to go!' I screamed.

'Twenty minutes,' said Graham. 'I've got a friend in Chalk Farm to come over. She's on her way. Twenty minutes.'

'I can't. I won't.'

'I'll pay you thirty quid.'

'How much?'

'All right, forty.'

Silence.

'Listen, you've been very good. I'll give you fifty pounds. How's that?'

Fifty pounds and he had me. The money was meaningless to him, it was small change. To me it was a week's wages. It was also more than I would get paid for a sketch from the BBC. More importantly, it was the price of my artistic integrity. My career hadn't even started and I had already sold out.

I took it out on Frank. It seemed only fair.

'Read me another story,' said Frank.

'Get lost.'

'I want to watch *Jackanory*.'

'Tough! We're watching the cricket!'

'I want to watch . . .'

'Shut up you little brat!'

He shut up, and remained shut up until Graham's friend from Chalk Farm arrived. I ran out of the house as she opened the door. I jumped on my bike, and pedalled like crazy all the way down to West London. The only way I could catch even the end of this meeting now was by going straight there in my gardening gear.

I ran into the BBC reception at three thirty. A man wearing a long overcoat and a hat that made him look like a spy ran up and grabbed me. I thought it was security, but it was Dick.

'Where the hell have you been?'

'What the hell are you wearing?'

'What am *I* wearing?' He was taking in my wellingtons and dirty trousers. 'When I said we should dress normally . . .'

We composed ourselves in the lift up to the fourth floor, the comedy department. Dick said, 'Don't crack any jokes, all right?'

'Why not?'

'Only amateur comedy writers makes jokes in meetings. We need to show the man we're serious, serious about comedy.'

The first thing the script editor said to us was, 'I'm afraid I've got to go to another meeting.' That could have been the truth – we were thirty minutes late – or it could have been a reaction to finding himself confronted by two young men with sombre faces, one dressed like a dustman, the other like Harry Lime, trying to convince him they were worthy of investment.

'What shows should we write for?' I asked as we followed him back to the lifts.

'Dave Allen,' said the script editor. 'He's doing a new series.' And then he went up and we went down.

Graham counted out the fifty pounds slowly, deliberately. 'Sorry about leaving you with Frank like that,' he said. 'I really needed you. Hope you didn't miss anything important.'

'No.'

'Good.'

Our relationship had changed now. I knew it and he knew it, and we both knew that the other knew it. I had thought I was in control, but he was. I had thought I had the power, but he had.

He smirked that smirk at me. He knew I had a price.

7

MAJOR CHESNEY

'House martins are late this year,' said Major Chesney. This may or may not have been true. The reason the remark was memorable was that he was looking at his watch when he made it.

'Going to be a warm summer,' he added, rocking back on his heels.

This was the great joy of working for Major Chesney: he was never anything less than a caricature. He had a stiff military moustache. His shoes were highly polished. He walked with his hands behind his back. He dressed like a tennis umpire in pale green and khaki. I never saw him without cufflinks. He had *The Times* delivered. He gave me instructions written down on a piece of A4 paper which had been folded and sliced with a ruler into quarters. His hobby was punctuality.

In fact, punctuality – his own and other people's – occupied a great deal of the major's time. I knew how the house martins felt. I had to get to his house on the dot of nine a.m. or I suffered the same reproach. If I arrived before, he wouldn't answer the door. After, and he'd greet me with a perfunctory 'Oh, it's you, is it?' and that unsubtle glance at his watch. He gave me a cup of tea at ten o'clock precisely. Then at eleven thirteen he would come out and inspect what I had done and say, 'I'll pay you by cheque if that's all right.' And I'd follow him into his study and stand at his desk, surrounded by his military memorabilia: medals, an assortment of army hats on a hatstand, a photograph of the major shaking hands with top brass. He'd hand me my cheque and I'd be out of the house by eleven fifteen and thirty seconds.

He wasn't a gardener himself. He would wave at the beds as if they were enemy territory. 'Mrs Chesney took care of it all,' he'd mumble. Gardening was like housework. All he wanted was a tidy view from his study desk. He was most concerned about his little lawn, and he owned a wonderful old push mower that he had serviced every year and which cut as well as any petrol-driven machine. He also had a variety of odd-looking tools for straightening and clipping the edges. He hinted that since his wife had died he'd rather lost interest in day-to-day matters. Perhaps the lawn helped him focus. He would peer at it for weeds, and prod at worm casts like a batsman flattening the pitch, and at the end of each session he'd pad across the grass in his shiny brogues and test it for springiness.

'You know, when someone dies, it's all paperwork,' he complained. And it was true he spent a lot of time in his study sorting through files, stapling and punching bits of paper, filing and refiling. It was endless but comforting work, it kept him busy.

Annie Kendal from across the road said the neighbours kept an eye out for him, but apart from that the only other soul in the major's life now was his Labrador, Carsons, with his dribbling jowl and back so bowed his stomach scraped the ground. I was Carsons's new best friend, and he'd limp round the garden after me, looking up with his milky eyes. 'I'm glad you've hit it off,' said the major. But Carsons was an old animal. His breathing had become a rasp, and his legs were prone to buckling. Once he leaned forward to sniff something in a flower bed and toppled over, flattening some dwarf hyacinths, and struggling to get to his feet. I told the major but he didn't seem to think it was anything to worry about. 'He'll be like this one minute and then be dashing across the Heath the next.' But Carsons hadn't dashed across the Heath for years and never would again.

To add to his general poor health, the dog was almost blind. I saw the major throw a ball for him, and Carsons didn't move, didn't even see it. The major grunted and said, 'I'd better get him some more tablets from the vet.' I imagined him dealing with his wife's illness the same way, denying it was happening – 'better get her some more tablets from the doc.' It was his way of dealing with the inevitable. With great effort he was managing to come to terms with the loss of his wife. The idea of losing Carsons as well wasn't worth contemplating.

Then one morning I called round and found the major in a state of excitement. A visitor was coming. 'Old army pal – Tommy Baines. Said he read about Mrs Chesney in the *Times* obits. Decided the least he could do was come and pay a visit.'

I asked the major if he would rather I came another day, but no, he insisted I work as usual. In fact I think he rather liked the idea of having Tommy Baines see his staff at work. His cleaning woman was already there complaining about having to cook lunch. I went into the garden and busied myself with the lawn, while the major sorted out bottles and decanters. It looked like he and Tommy were going to have a session.

Tommy Baines duly arrived, and while the major was clearly overjoyed to see an old friend he wasn't half as happy as Carsons. Tommy Baines, bless him, had brought along his spaniel, and you've never seen an invalid perk up the way Carsons did as the prim little bitch flaunted her big ears and walked across the lawn, going straight past him to the secluded area behind the shed. He couldn't have seen her properly, but he could recognise the scent of a woman just as well now as he could in his youth. He had the look of Terry-Thomas – 'I say. Ding dong!' – as he followed her down the garden path.

'Snifter?' offered the major.

'Scotch, I think,' said Tommy Baines.

'Good idea,' said the major and they settled on the terrace with the French windows open. Tommy talked about his journey for a full hour, which must have been longer than it took him to travel from Stevenage. The major countered with a detailed knowledge of the street plan of 1940s Palermo, and then an invitation to Tommy to tell his story of the German sniper and the bottle of HP sauce. Tommy managed to spin the tale out until a good part of the bottle of Scotch had disappeared. At noon the cleaner rang the dinner gong. 'Ah, time for drinks,' said Tommy.

Carsons meanwhile was still behind the shed with his visitor, proving that, in fact, you can teach an old dog new tricks. Even the smell of dinner didn't distract him. I left as the major began moving the salt and pepper round the table and rearranging the dessertspoons to recreate the pincer movement his regiment employed in North Africa.

I didn't disturb him for my cheque. It was reward enough to see both him and Carsons in action, the excitement of their youth bringing the blood to their faces again.

I did jobs for a number of elderly people. Some were happy, healthy couples who sat on their verandas and listened to plays on the radio together. They hadn't much to say to each other, but there was someone there to say it to if they ever felt the need. Most elderly clients, however, were like the major and having to manage on their own, and in their own way: for every Major Chesney who had retreated behind a stiff upper lip, there was a Mrs Fleming, who did what she liked and said whatever came into her head. One day a Jehovah's Witness knocked on her door and said he was speaking to people in the neighbourhood on the subject of a world without violence. She hit him with a rolled-up copy of the *Radio Times*.

Some elderly clients were extremely wary of me, watching every move I made from behind lace curtains, and they locked the door as soon as I left. Others didn't really care what I did in the garden, they just wanted someone to talk out loud to for two hours. I didn't have to listen, all they required was a human within earshot. I was probably as good as a visit from Social Services for them.

For many a lack of money was the primary concern. Mr Sweeney, who lived in a little garden flat in West Hampstead, spent most of his time trying to stretch his savings. He wasn't only concerned about his own shortages, though. He was a champion of the elderly, and age hadn't dimmed any anger he felt towards the system. 'Old people want respect, that's all,' he said. 'But people stopped respecting me the day I stopped working.'

I found that hard to believe. Here was a man defined by

his energy. He said he never slept; he read all night, not books though, 'haven't got time for books, life's too short.' He devoured newspapers and magazines and was so well informed on current affairs that if you asked him a question on anything from human rights violations in El Salvador to test-tube babies, you got a thirty-minute reply that could have come straight out of the *Economist*. The plight of the elderly was what annoyed him most. I only worked an hour a week for him, but getting away at the end of the session took another hour as he railed at how pathetic state pensions were, how people who fought in the war were living off cat food, how a seventy-year-old down the road had waited two years for a hip replacement: 'He'll be dead before his turn comes – of course that's the idea.'

I had dropped my prices as low as I could as soon as I saw the state of the cardigan Mr Sweeney was wearing. And after I got to know him better I suggested maybe a gardener was a luxury he couldn't afford. But he yelled at me, 'Why shouldn't I have a gardener? I'm seventy-five years old! I can't bend over. I've earned the right to employ a gardener.'

He wrote letters to borough councils demanding improved wheelchair access. He helped raise money for research into Parkinson's. He got people to sign petitions for pension reform. He wrote long letters to his MP about prescription charges. He said, 'Injustice keeps me going.'

When he discovered I wanted to be a writer he shook his head. 'You don't seem the sort.'

'What sort?'

'Passionate sort. You have to have passion to write.'

'I can be passionate.'

'What kind of upbringing did you have?'

'Why?'

'Hemingway said, "The best thing a writer can have is an unhappy childhood."'

Damn it. I'd had a happy, middle-class childhood on the Dorset coast; no broken home, no abuse, no poverty.

'To be a writer,' said Sweeney, 'you have to want to change things, and to change things . . .' here he narrowed his eyes, 'you have to be desperate!'

I tried to gauge how desperate I was, and the answer made me feel as though I should forget about writing there and then and get a job in W.H. Smith.

One day I found Sweeney in a very excitable mood, making piles of sandwiches. 'Going on a protest march,' he said, proudly.

'Protest march against what?'

He had to think for a moment, then said, 'Reform of the state pension.'

It poured with rain, but he had a wonderful day. 'Did you see us on TV?' he asked later. He showed me the pictures in the paper, a long line of pensioners in macs and head-scarves, braving the conditions to deliver a petition to Downing Street.

'Direct action is the only way to make some people take notice,' he said with satisfaction.

But then a week later he seemed grumpy and depressed. A government spokesman had announced no changes to the pension during the next term. 'It made no difference,' Sweeney said sadly. 'All those signatures and they're just going to ignore us. That's what happens to the elderly, we get patted on the head like dogs.' He kicked a cardboard box across the lawn.

'Give it time,' I said.

'I haven't got time,' he said pathetically.

I'd never seen him like this before. It was as if he'd had

enough. I wondered whether I should tell a neighbour. But then as I left I saw him sitting in the kitchen, chuckling, making notes on a scrap of paper.

'I've just had a great idea,' he said.

Eventually I met Lady Brignal. So many people had spoken about her good bones I'd come to think of her as a skeleton, someone who would make a tasty stock if you boiled her up. I suppose I was bound to be disappointed when I saw her in the flesh. I found myself peering at her, trying to work out which of her bones were the ones that impressed people so much. I noticed she kept her distance from me.

But she said she was pleased with the way the garden was looking, and she was keen to clear up the rockery and plant some Alpines. She asked me to go to the nursery and buy £5 worth. Helen would drive me.

Helen had good bones too, I thought, as I sat in the passenger seat. In fact, if I had to choose, I preferred Helen's bones to Lady Brignal's. Since our walk on the Heath we had become more wary of each other. Or at least, she had become more wary of me. She still played her music as I gardened, but didn't open the window for me to hear.

She was a tense driver. She sat stiffly and gripped the wheel with white knuckles. I suggested to her that instead of cleaning and gardening we should start an agency for cleaners and gardeners. We could ask my friend Pete to come in with us and include decorators.

She didn't like that idea, though. 'We'd earn too much money,' she said.

'What's wrong with that?'

'We're supposed to be struggling.'

Her point was that it was hard enough trying to be a writer or an actor as it was. If we had a money-spinning alternative to turn to, it would be too tempting; we'd sell out.

Once again my commitment was being questioned. I told her how I was worried my happy childhood spent on the beach might have left me too well adjusted to be a writer. 'What sort of upbringing did your boyfriend have?' I asked her.

'His parents abandoned him when he was two and he spent the rest of his childhood in foster homes until he was fourteen, when he ran away and got a job in a Soho strip club.'

Typical.

I said, 'Maybe I need to get married and have a family and then behave badly and abandon them so I can write about my guilt.'

She shrugged, determined not to be amused.

She waited outside the garden centre while I went in and asked Bernie the manager to gather together a selection of his finest Alpines. Bernie had become my official supplier over the last couple of months. He was keen to encourage my business. He even let me put an advert on his notice board, and had taken it upon himself to be my advisor in all things horticultural. When he saw me sorting through the bunches of cut flowers at the cash desk he said, 'Got a lady friend?'

'No.'

'Who's that in the car then?'

'A person to whom I'm not altogether unattracted.'

'If you want to dazzle a lady only roses will do.'

'I don't want to dazzle her, I want to . . . intrigue her, slightly.'

Bernie thought about this. 'Freesias will do the job.'

'I thought they were cattle.'

'Freesias are the sort of flower you want to give to someone you aren't sure about.'

'It's not that I'm not sure about her, I just don't want her thinking I've not got any number of women I can turn to if she rejects me.'

Bernie thought harder. 'In that case I recommend phlox.'

'Too uninteresting, and too hard to spell.'

'Lupins.'

'Too industrial.'

'A house plant?'

'Who do you think I am?'

'Tulips.'

'Silly flowers.'

Then he clicked his fingers. 'Cut-price tulips.'

'Now you're talking.'

I went back to the car and put the box of Alpines in the boot, then presented Helen with the tulips.

She looked startled. 'What are you doing?'

'I bought these for you.'

'Why?'

'I don't know. It's all right, they were on offer.'

She tried not to smile but couldn't help it. She even blushed a little. 'Thanks,' she mumbled, and started the engine.

On the way back she said, 'I wouldn't worry about not having a grim childhood. I don't think it's important.'

'You reckon.'

'My boyfriend writes plays about social realism so upsetting that at the end of them he always has to put the number for a helpline.'

Her implication was that thirty-second comedy sketches for television weren't inspired by unresolved personal trauma. They were lightweight. I wasn't sure, though. Good, original comedy came from looking at things from an obtuse angle, and for that a warped point of view was a bonus.

Take Mr Sweeney, for example. There was no-one with a point of view more warped than his, and he was a source of wonderful and humorous ideas, none better than his latest one. He had a plan to solve his pension problems for good: he was going to turn to crime.

'What crime?' I said, laughing.

'Securicor van,' he said, not laughing at all.

'You can't turn to crime.'

'Why not?'

'Because . . .'

'Because I'm an old man? You were going to say because I'm an old man, weren't you?'

'No.'

'Why should the young have the monopoly on crime? Why should it only be youth who drive round in getaway cars and put stockings over their heads?'

'But . . . a Securicor van?'

'Maybe a building society, I don't know. I'll speak to Vic.'

Vic was his partner on the pensions protest and on the campaign for reduced prescription charges. Now he became his partner in crime. Vic would come round and they'd plot together over the kitchen table.

I said to them, 'What are you going to do if you get caught?'

'I'll plead dementia,' said Sweeney. The plan appealed to him so much because it was advantageous to be old.

'It doesn't matter if they do convict us,' said Vic. 'They're not going to imprison a man in his late seventies.'

He'd been reading how prisons hated having elderly inmates with prostate problems.

'They can give me ten years if they like,' said Sweeney. 'I'll be dead in two.'

Vic said, 'The beauty of being old is we've got nothing to lose. We should do the big one now.'

They got a lot of fun out of the idea. They went to the library to do research. They walked up and down the Finchley Road choosing their building society. It became a hobby.

But then they abandoned their plans as quickly as they had taken them up. Vic's blood pressure had become raised, Sweeney explained, 'The excitement of an armed robbery is giving him palpitations.'

I tried not to laugh. For the first time it seemed as if Sweeney wasn't taking himself seriously. He shook his head and said, 'I thought we might inspire a chain reaction, you know. Pensioners up and down the country would be holding up Securicor vans, just taking what they deserved. Shame really.'

I had hardly ever been up on Hampstead Heath before I started gardening, but now I carried a detailed map of its tracks and woods around in my head.

It was the window through which I noticed the seasons slowly change. Spring had arrived whether anyone was ready for it or not. It needed no planting or husbandry, it just turned up about the same time every year. But now the blossom had blown away. There was the splash of someone swimming across one of the lidos, and I knew summer was on the way when I heard Mungo Jerry coming from a jogger's Walkman.

The paths down by the ponds became busy with young mothers wheeling their infants about. Among them one sunny afternoon I came across Annie Kendal and her newborn. But she shook her head gravely when I waved at her. 'Have you heard?' she said.

The news in her road was that old Carsons had passed away. The major had come down in the morning and not been able to open the kitchen door and found Carsons slumped against it. The dog was still alive but unable to move. The vet was called and Carsons was taken away, but he never returned.

The neighbours had rallied round. They took meals in for the major, they fussed over him. 'He's finding it very quiet,' Annie said. 'He needs to have as much company as he can.'

He took a while to answer his door, and when he did come he stood there with a napkin in his hand and a crumb of cheese on his moustache. Then I noticed he had slippers on instead of shoes, which was such an aberration I knew he wasn't himself.

I said I was sorry to hear about Carsons. He nodded and dabbed his mouth and mumbled something about pickled onions.

It felt strange to be working in the major's garden without the hulk of Carsons nudging up against my leg – 'Go on give me a pat, go on, go on.' I smiled when I remembered the date with Tommy Baines's spaniel. Maybe that had been what pushed him over the edge.

I did the lawn and the edges as usual. The major came outside at eleven thirteen and said, 'It's all right if I pay you by cheque, isn't it?'

I went inside and stood by his desk, noticing that Carsons memorabilia had taken its place alongside that of the major's regiment and his late wife. A picture of Carsons as a dashing young stud was on the sideboard next to Mrs Chesney dressed for the ball. I watched the major write out my cheque with his frail hand, and it just seemed so unfair that he had to deal with crises like these at a time in his life when he was least physically and emotionally equipped to do so.

'Will you get another dog?' I asked.

He looked at me as though I'd just danced on Carsons's grave. But then he said, 'People keep asking me that.'

'It's nice to have a pet.'

'Of course, Mrs Chesney used to have a cat. Marmalade sort of thing. But I'm not a cat person. I used to think — good drop kick and it'll be over the hedge.' He looked out of the window, trying to roll back time. 'I remember Carsons used to get great sport terrifying the living daylights out of the chap,' and he laughed at the thought of the youthful Carsons chasing the cat over garden walls.

'Have you thought of fish?' I said.

'I beg your pardon?'

'Tropical fish, in a tank, very relaxing.'

He looked at me as if I was nuts.

'A budgie, parrot?'

'Damned annoying things.'

'Tortoise?'

'I don't think so,' and he glanced at the picture of himself and Carsons out on the moor: he in shooting breeches with a gun broken over his arm, and Carsons by his side in a nimrod-like pose. 'I'm a dog man, you see.'

The problem was solved thanks to the neighbours. They had told him he should get another dog, but he was reluctant to have a puppy which would outlive him and then become a burden on someone.

'So we suggested he give a home to something from the Dog Rescue,' Annie Kendal told me. She had taken the major down to the pound. She'd expected him to go for nothing less than a pedigree, but he'd seen this little black and tan cross that had been found abandoned a few weeks previously and had only days to go until it got the needle. The major had refused to leave without it.

I saw the two of them walking down the road a couple

of days later. The major had his walking stick and was wearing a flat cap, and he was blowing his cheeks out trying to keep up with this cheeky little dog that moved down the pavement like a vacuum cleaner.

I waved and the major waved back and was almost tugged off balance as he was towed towards the Heath. It looked like a nervous rascal of a dog. I imagined it being someone's gift the previous Christmas, then being ignored as the novelty wore off, clouted for peeing on the floor, locked up all day, shouted at, turned out when the family decided to go on holiday, then walking the streets until the police caught it and put it on death row.

And I thought: even that scabby little mongrel is better qualified to be a writer than I am.

SUMMER

8

BARCLAYS BANK

Dick and I sat in a room above a pub in the middle of Hackney Marshes, and tried to think of sketches for Dave Allen.

But we sat in silence, blocked. 'It's no good,' said Dick. 'I need to have Dave Allen here if I'm going to write for him. I mean it's the least he could do.'

A bee buzzed through the window into the room and landed on a Chinese takeaway menu. Dick threw an Elmore Leonard paperback at it and it flew out again.

'Why would Dave Allen want to come out to a pub in the Hackney Marshes?'

'There's a stripper on at seven.'

'Really?'

'Yeah.'

We sat in silence again, until Dick said, 'Alison. That's her name. She comes from Theydon Bois.'

'I've never met anyone from Theydon Bois.'

'She's going to be a nurse.'

'It's shameful. Nurses having to supplement their income . . .'

'No, she's going to dress up as a nurse.'

We sat in silence again, trying to think of Dave Allen, trying not to think of nurses.

'The evenings are getting longer,' said Neil. 'A time for reflection.' Then he took my hand and said as gently as he could, 'I don't want to discourage you, but your writing career seems like a mistake. Perhaps you should pack it up and get yourself a proper job.'

'Like, in the mortgage business?'

'You're my friend. Say the word and I'll fix it.'

He was serious, and I believed he was trying to be helpful. He would have loved to see me put on a suit and go to the office every morning. He would probably have lowered my rent. Neil was the sort of person who couldn't understand why anyone would want to sponsor an artist, but would happily subsidise someone training for an enlightened career in merchant banking.

What Neil wasn't to know was that I had recently taken a job in the banking business, at the Swiss Cottage branch of Barclays in fact. I had been summoned there by the manager, who led me down an alleyway beside the building and up some steps to emerge on a flat roof that contained a large flower bed in a brick enclosure. There was a walkway all around, and benches at regular intervals, so that the whole effect was one of coming across an oasis, a place of respite for the beleaguered office workers of the Finchley Road.

Potentially so, anyway. Because it was in a state, neglected for years. The tips of some rose bushes could be seen as they reached for the sky, but the place was above all a tribute to the exceptional variety of weeds that will grow in the city no matter how much concrete covers them.

'I want it to be a retreat for the staff to come during their breaks this summer,' said the manager. 'I want it to be . . . soothing.'

A tough job, but I was willing to take it. He asked for a quote, something I'd never done before — normally I just charged by the hour. I quickly tried to work out how long it would take to clear the rubbish out and encourage what was left to reclaim the plot. I reckoned four mornings of four hours — sixteen times £1.50, plus a bit extra.

'Twenty-five pounds,' I said.

He looked at me, suspiciously. 'Twenty-five pounds?'

'That's right.'

'For the whole lot?'

'Yeah.'

'No extras?'

'No.'

'The job's yours.'

He told me I'd find a 'wheelbarrow and stuff' in the janitor's shed, then he was hurrying away as fast as he could and I realised I could have asked fifty pounds and he'd have been just as happy.

I started the following Monday morning. I went to work with all the commuters, head down, hurrying along the Finchley Road. But as they descended into the Underground I went up to this secret garden.

I soon discovered it had been planted with some thought. A variety of shrubs emerged, and as I cleared the under-growth from around them the daylight was like the kiss of life. They all but sighed as they regained consciousness.

For the first hour I was on my own, but then staff surfaced from the surrounding offices on their breaks. Some came with files to read, some with newspapers, others to sit and squint in the sunshine and drink coffee from plastic cups. They sat on the benches around the garden and watched me, as if I was performing – gardening as a one-man-show. No-one spoke to me, but they all stared, some thinking: 'I'd give anything for a job like that,' others: 'Poor sod, what a way to make a living.'

I got used to them after a while, like animals do at the zoo. They were just part of the space, and slowly I found myself watching them as much as they watched me. Office life was being played out before me. As the week got warmer the secretaries pulled their dresses up a couple of inches to catch the sun on their legs. The junior managers strolled out, jackets slung over their shoulders, ties loosened. They sat and poked each other, dared one another to ask a secretary out. Then came the middle managers, men whose bellies had grown as their hair had receded. There had been a time when they would have sat nearer the secretaries, but now they settled for the crossword. The executives came out last. They sat apart. They spoke in whispers. They drank their coffee in a hurry and were gone.

Then one of my audience surprised me by speaking to me. He was an Indian lad, sitting on his own drinking a can of Coke. He wore a pale blue turban and had a big gold ring. 'What you doing?' he asked.

'I'm doing the garden. What do you think I'm doing?'

He grinned and nodded, as if I'd let him in on the secret. 'Why?'

'I . . .' I couldn't think why. 'They asked me to.'

'They paying you?'

'Course they're paying me.'

'How much?'

'£25.'

He shrugged. 'Not bad.'

His name was Balbir. He worked in the post room of a recruitment agency. 'Up there,' he said and he pointed up to a floor in the clouds. 'I earn £90 a week, before tax. My cousin got me the job.'

Balbir had only recently arrived in England. He was going to North London Polytechnic in September to study Economics.

'Have you seen *10*?' he asked me.

'*10*. The movie?'

'Yeah. Bo Derek and Dudley Moore.'

'No.'

'I've heard it's very good. Very sexy.'

'I heard that as well.'

He took a deep breath and said quietly, 'I'm going to go and see it with that girl over there on that bench.'

He pointed over to a group of three secretaries sitting on a bench together drinking coffee.

'Which one?'

'The one on the left, the Indian girl.'

She was about the same age as Balbir, short and pretty. She was eating a tub of yoghurt very gracefully.

'Lucky you,' I said.

'I haven't asked her yet.'

'Oh.'

He emptied his can of Coke. He was nervous. He was building up courage to go and ask her.

'I'll wait till her friends go in. Do you think she'll go Dutch?'

'Go what?'

'Dutch.'

It was such a long time since I'd heard the expression I wondered where he'd got it from. 'You mean, will she pay for herself?'

'Yes.'

'I don't know. I suppose so,' and I realised one of the reasons he was so nervous was that he wasn't sure how to ask someone out in England. He was frightened of making a blunder. I said, 'Of course, you could . . . treat her.'

'Why?'

'Well . . .'

'She'll think I'm rich if I do that. I have to be very careful with money. I told you, I'm going to the North London Polytechnic in September.'

'She might just think you're generous. Or that you like her.'

'She's going inside.'

The secretaries got up and walked back to the office. Balbir made a move, but then lost his nerve and sat down again. He slumped. 'I can't do this.'

'I can't do this,' said Dick, later that afternoon. I sat staring at the floor. He lay staring at the ceiling. Working for Dave Allen was killing us.

I looked round the room, searching for something that might inspire a sketch: a Superman comic, a bottle of Musk for Men, a sock. There was one shelf in the room and it was fifty per cent dust, fifty per cent science fiction. On the table was a coffee cup that had mould growing in it. I looked out of the window and saw a cloud the shape of Australia.

'Trouble is I don't really like Dave Allen,' said Dick. 'Too mainstream.'

'What do we know about him?'

'He's Irish.'

'He used to work at Butlin's.'

'He's lost half a finger?'

'Which finger?'

'I don't know. What difference does it make?'

'I don't know.'

I switched on the TV. A sports reporter was talking about a heavyweight legend who was to challenge for 'the big one'.

I switched channels. 'The Pope is to visit Ireland,' said the newsreader.

That evening we wrote a sketch about a boxer who decides to challenge the Pope for his title, Pontifex Maximus. 'I'm aware he's God's representative on Earth,' said the boxer to the interviewer, 'but I think I can take him in five.'

We were very pleased with it. We put it in an envelope and both walked down to the post box and almost reluctantly sent it on its way, not wanting to part with something so perfect. Moments like that glowed with promise. They made us want to stay up all night. They were the occasions when it seemed that a good comedy sketch, like a good poem, could change everything.

I had managed to keep out of Powerflowers' way since that first meeting. But we worked the same patch; we were bound to cross paths again.

The next time was one morning when I was working at Mrs Lavenham's. I was securing a net over her cherry tree. She let the birds have a week feasting on it first, then she covered it and let the rest of the fruit ripen for her own use, and for mine. She gave me bagfuls – big dark red cherries, bursting with juice.

I had secured a net around the tree when I began to hear activity next door. Power tools screamed into life, cement mixers wound themselves up. I peered over and there were Powerflowers performing a horticultural lobotomy. Everything in the garden was cut back to the ground. Trellis was nailed to every fence. Creosote was liberally slapped on, and then concrete plastered over whatever was left. That was that. Job done.

Don, the driver I'd confronted before, grinned when he saw me. 'Oh look, it's the competition.'

The others appeared at the fence. They wore cut-off jeans in the heat, and big boots. They reminded me of pirates.

'We don't bother with hoeing weeds,' said one.

'We use bark chips instead,' said another.

'We smother 'em. Huh.'

'How much do you get paid?' asked the one with his arse hanging out of his shorts.

I told him my hourly rate and he laughed. 'We get double that.'

Then another said, 'Do you ever get your end away?'

'What?'

'You know, does the lady of the house ever pay you in kind?'

'Er . . .'

'He doesn't even get his end away.' He laughed. 'Norman here gets his end away all the time.'

Norman had removed his green T-shirt. He had muscles where all the others had belly, and he had permed hair. He said, 'Who you working for?'

'Mrs Lavenham.'

'Is she knockable?'

'What?'

'Is she fit?'

'As a matter of fact she's got arthritis.'

That put him off.

They asked me where else I worked. I said here and there, then proudly told them I had a contract at Barclays Bank on the Finchley Road. At this news Don lost his smile.

'That roof garden?'

'Yes.'

He stared at me, wondering if I was bluffing. 'We looked at that. We gave him a price.'

'Your price wasn't good enough, was it?'

If he could have torn the fence down and grabbed me, I think he would have. Instead he started his drill up again and mouthed a bunch of threats.

I thought no more about them. The following day I went back to Barclays and spent the morning pruning the shrubs. I noticed Balbir's girlfriend come out with her friends and sit on their usual bench. Shortly afterwards Balbir appeared.

He said to me, 'My friend Neville went to see *10*. He says it was about one man's desire for the impossible dream, and his ultimate realisation that he was better off without it.'

'Mmm.'

'Do you think it's a good film to see on a first date?'

'I would say it's perfect.'

'Good.'

'Have you asked her?'

'No.'

'Why not?'

He shrugged. 'I've a feeling she's going to say no.'

'She might say yes.'

He drank from his can, crushed it, and then said to me, 'I want you to do me a favour. I want you to ask her out for me.'

'Get lost.'

'Please.'

'No.'

'Why not? We do it at home all the time.'

'I don't believe you.'

'We always ask girls out for each other. That way you never get rejected.'

'I'm not asking her out for you. I don't even know her.'

'Neither do I.'

'You expect me to go over there and ask her if she'll go out with you to the pictures and pay for herself?'

'Yes.'

'If I ask her I'll ask her to go with me.'

He rubbed his knees, tapped his feet. 'She's got lovely hands,' he said. 'Her hands were what first attracted me to her.'

I told him, 'You'll regret it for ever if you don't ask her.'

'I need an excuse to speak to her.'

'Maybe you could start a fire in the office and then make sure you're the one to rescue her . . .'

'I've thought of that. I've also thought of stealing something from her handbag, and then following her home and seeing where she lives and knocking on her door and giving it to her and saying she dropped it and then starting a conversation . . .'

'I've seen that film.'

'*Marathon Man* with Dustin Hoffman.'

She and her friends were giggling now. One of them was looking over our way. I said to Balbir, 'They're talking about you. They know you fancy her.'

'How do they know?'

'Because every day you come out at exactly the same time as they do and sit here looking at her with your tongue hanging out.'

They got up to go, but then Balbir's girlfriend stayed, opened a magazine and sat there. 'Go on!' I hissed at him. 'She's waiting for you.'

But he delayed and delayed, and presently she put her magazine in her bag and went back inside.

He seemed relieved. 'Maybe tomorrow.'

I finished the patch I was doing. The manager came out and noticed a rosebud was about to bloom. 'Look, a flower,' he said, with as much rhapsody as a Barclays branch manager can muster. 'Good work.'

I felt a rush of pride. I had tamed this wilderness with my trowel and pruning saw, and it was about to reward me with a single rose.

I packed up and went down the stairs to the alley where I kept my bike. But there was something not quite right about it, it took me a moment to realise what – both wheels were missing.

I had no proof Powerflowers were the culprits, of course – the alley was easily accessed by anyone – but it was a joke to think someone would steal the wheels and not the bike. Who else could it be? I thought about reporting it to the police, but in the end I went down to the bike shop in Kentish Town and bought two new wheels. The shopkeeper knocked off two quid when I told him the old ones had been stolen, but they still cost half of what I'd earned at Barclays all week.

I felt angry and stupid, to have thought I could take them on.

'They're just bullies,' said Helen. 'You need to stand up to them.'

'There are five of them!'

'So?' She had a fire in her eyes; a determination I'd never seen before.

'So . . . they'll leave me lying in a ditch somewhere.'

'So!'

'So . . .'

And she launched herself: 'You can't let them get the better of you. You have to fight for what you believe is right. You have to stand up and follow your heart. The rewards will come if you persevere . . . if you are true to yourself.'

'. . .'

'. . .'

'You've got a job, haven't you?'

'Yes.'

'What job?'

'I'm a tomato.'

She was telling the truth. She was a tomato in a children's TV show where she had to lie on top of another actor who was dressed up as a hamburger patty, and then be lain on by another actor who wore the top half of a bun costume. To complete the burger they all lay on top of the poor guy dressed as the bottom half of the bun.

The job had given her confidence, made her bullish, justified all the cleaning and dog-walking.

'Congratulations,' I said.

'I've earned it. It's what you get if you're determined never to give up, to stand firm when all around you . . .'

'Yeah, yeah, all right.'

I spent the last morning at Barclays dressing the bed with peat. When I'd finished it all looked a little exposed, but there was room for the plants to do something now. The single rose had bloomed. It was a watery pink and it looked fragile in the wind that some days gusted round the buildings.

Balbir came out as usual and sat and waited for his girlfriend. He said, 'Today's the day. I'm going to do it today. I've got to do it today.'

'Why today?'

'It's the last day of the movie.'

It didn't seem as though she was going to show. He drank two cans of Coke. He shuffled his feet nervously. Then out she came, and this time she was on her own.

'Nothing can stop you now,' I said to Balbir.

'You're right. Nothing.'

He breathed deeply. He tried to swallow but his mouth was dry.

She didn't even have a magazine with her this time. She was sitting there with her legs crossed, sitting on her lovely hands, looking at the sky.

'But I can't just . . . go over there.'

'Don't start this again.'

'I need to offer her something?'

'Offer her a ticket to the cinema.'

'I told you, I'm going to North London Polytechnic.'

I looked at him. I looked at her. They needed to be together. They needed to be in the back row of the cinema.

I took my secateurs and clipped the single rose. The whole garden seemed to scream.

I handed the flower to Balbir. 'Don't screw up.'

He stiffened; he knew there was no way out now. He got to his feet, emboldened, and he strode the long way round the garden to her. She saw him coming and looked away, but he went straight up to her and offered her the flower. She laughed, then took it and smelt it and let him sit down beside her.

He looked very formal, his back very straight. They spoke for a while. He pointed to somewhere in the distance, maybe the cinema. The sun came out and she shielded her eyes with one of her lovely hands. Then they got up and strolled to the door. He held it open for her.

Before I left the manager came out and admired the

finished job, until he noticed the rose was gone. I pleaded ignorance.

'Vandals!' he spat. 'Damn vandals! You do something nice for them and this is how they repay you! They don't deserve it.'

But I felt vindicated. I had cultivated something at last. I had grown a flower, and it had been put to the best possible use. I liked to think of Balbir and his new girlfriend watching the film on Saturday night, at the start of a long relationship that saw him through his time at North London Polytechnic and then produced three children and a happy home, and all because of one pale pink rose.

9

CHRIS & MARTINA

London was floored by a heatwave. Commuters had damp patches under their arms by nine a.m. In Ealing a bus conductor got sent home for working in his swimming trunks. Each morning milk soured on the doorstep. Each evening the smell of barbecued meat drifted across back gardens. If there was nothing good on TV, Neil and I would sit by the open kitchen window and listen to the Welsh couple next door argue into the night.

Hampstead Heath hardened and cracked. Sunbathers spread out on the slopes and burnt their eyelids. Well-fed pedigree dogs lay under trees, panting. An ice-cream salesman lost his temper and yelled at some Dutch tourists. I cycled to work every morning under a china blue sky and returned when it was a dirty brown.

'There'll be a hosepipe ban any day now,' said Nugent. There would be if he carried on watering his entire plot to saturation point day and night. Every container he owned, from water butts to milk bottles, was filled in readiness for the inevitable rationing.

Gardens sighed in such unfamiliar heat. Lawns wilted and grew dusty; birdbaths dried out; flowers in hanging baskets fell to their knees like men lost in the desert. I developed a labourer's suntan.

It was a flaming June and I had a job at a house off Spaniards Road, where I gardened to the sound of piano music that drifted through open French windows. And this was no recording. This was my employer, Kenneth, rippling over the keys of the grand in his music room. He made a living as a composer and he played all morning, producing such achingly beautiful tunes that they drew me towards the house. 'What's that called?' I'd ask.

'It's not called anything,' he'd say. 'It's an advert for a petrol company.'

He wrote beautiful music for the ugliest things: this dreamy tune for a packet of crisps, that sparkling melody for a new cough mixture. He said he never became attached to anything he wrote; he didn't care what happened to a piece after it left his house. 'They can do what they like with it,' he said. He even claimed he never recognised his music when he saw or heard the finished commercial. He'd abandoned it by then.

His music became the soundtrack to my gardening. When he played *piano* I gently clipped the hedge; *forte*, and I dug the spade in and turned over a bed with gusto; *allegro* and I ran the wheelbarrow down the path until he struck a *crescendo* and there was nothing else I could do but dump the whole lot onto the compost.

Music provided Kenneth with a good life. His flat was large and airy, part of a rambling converted property, and the garden had a mysterious Victorian ambience with a path that wound into every corner. The trees were too big really, so that the lawn had grown mossy beneath them, but this just added to the lush character of it all, and in the heatwave this was as shady and cool a refuge as anywhere in London.

One day I was at the bottom of the plot, cutting back some brambles. If I did hear the whistling of a heavy object hurtling through the trees above I didn't pay it any attention, until it landed at my feet with a dry thud. I looked down and saw a cricket ball.

That's odd, I thought. But not that odd. The cricket season was well under way. I pushed through the undergrowth to the fence and found myself gazing onto the playing fields of Highgate School. A pavilion stood at the far end. A groundsman sitting on a giant mower patrolled the outfield. Nearer were some boys practising in nets. I thought about throwing the ball back to them, but they didn't seem to be showing any interest. So I kept it – an unlikely souvenir of Highgate.

Over the rest of the morning I found a half-dozen of the things, of various ages. They'd been falling through the trees for years. Before I left I presented them all to Kenneth. He took one look and said, 'You have them. I hate cricket,' and he turned his nose up as if I was offering him a cheese he found suspicious. 'Not my game, I'm afraid,' he added. I assumed he wasn't the sporty sort, but that wasn't the case. 'I'm a tennis fan,' he said, and he threw an imaginary tennis ball in the air and whacked it with an imaginary racquet and it went sailing out of the imaginary court.

Just how much of a tennis fan he was I was about to discover, because the following week Wimbledon Fortnight began and Kenneth's schedule, indeed his whole life, changed. I was at his house on the opening day of the tournament, the sun still blazing, the earth as parched as the previous week. In place of music coming from his workroom, however, now I could

103

hear the sound of tennis balls being hit, and the soft tones of Dan Maskell interrupted by frequent yelps from Kenneth as he applauded or groaned at a shot.

I got to work on the lawn. It was bumpy now and cracks were opening up in it. I took my shirt off and started clipping the edges. Suddenly there was a voice at my side: 'Lemon barley water,' and there was Kenneth in a panama hat and long-sleeved cotton shirt, carrying a tray of drinks. I reached instinctively for my T-shirt. He smiled and poured me a drink and one for himself. 'I have to cover up in the sun,' he said. 'Fair skin.'

'Yes.'

'I don't go brown. I just peel.'

'Yes.'

'Cheers.'

'Cheers,' I said. And our glasses kissed briefly.

'Tell me,' said Kenneth. 'Do you like Chris or Martina?'

'I beg your pardon?'

'Chris Evert or Martina Navratilova?'

Ah, the lady tennis players: the favourite Chris Evert, the girl next door whom the British had adopted, or the newcomer Martina Navratilova, the Czech athlete, who was harder and meaner and no respecter of reputations. Kenneth waited for my reply with a face that said: think carefully before you answer.

'I like . . . Chris,' I said.

'So do I,' said Kenneth, relieved that I had made the right choice. 'She's powerful though, that Martina, and Chrissie has to lose sometime . . .'

He was showing an even keener interest than usual this year, because he had a ticket for the final. He wanted Chris to be there and so he was rallying support. A round of applause from the TV sent him hurrying inside. 'Chris is playing her first-round match,' he called. 'Do you want to watch for a bit?'

His living room was all white: white carpet, walls, ceiling, piano. It didn't matter where I sat, or even stood, I was going to leave a muddy mark. I perched on the edge of a chair that looked as if it had been made by a team of scientists working in isolation in Scandinavia.

Kenneth said, 'I've got no time for men's tennis. They just stand there and slug it out. Connors is so boorish, and as for Borg – all that bumfluff.'

The ladies by comparison were personalities. They were approachable. 'Chris Evert is the sort of girl you find serving at Boots,' said Kenneth. 'Don't you love that hairdo, so natural.'

She did look beautifully summery, and Kenneth purred as Chris breezed through the first set against some French schoolgirl.

I noticed that the piano had its lid down. Work had stopped for the fortnight and tennis had taken over. Before, when he sat at his piano or when he strolled around with a tune in his head, he seemed in such control of himself and everything around him; he could block out any distraction. But now he was fussing about with drinks, chewing his nails, sitting forward on the white couch to applaud any shot Chris made. He seemed suddenly very vulnerable with his fair skin and little feet.

Chris Evert won the match with speed and ease. Kenneth looked a lot more tired at the end than she did. 'I'm going to have to have a lie-down,' he said, and I went back to my edges.

Kenneth wasn't my only client with a ticket for a big game that week. Mrs Lloyd who lived on the Holly Lodge Estate also had one, but hers wasn't for the tennis. She was getting warmed up for the Lord's Test Match – England versus India.

She'd been following the previous matches in the series on the radio all month. She had earned this little luxury, she told me. Her children had grown up and had children of their own. Her husband spent all day at the office steering home their pension. If she wanted to settle down and enjoy a day in the company of the team from *Test Match Special*, then she jolly well would.

Mrs Lloyd's garden was small and uncluttered with a well-cared-for shed and fence, and a lot of paving stone for ground cover. I spent the time hoeing weed-free beds, mowing a bald lawn, treating for non-existent greenfly. She was obsessive about having stakes in the beds to support the flowers. She didn't like to stand for long periods herself these days, and maybe she felt sympathy. Hers was one of those gardens where I didn't really understand why I was employed. It was usually a status thing – you had to have a gardener the way you had to have a window cleaner, although the idea that I could improve someone's standing in the neighbourhood made me laugh. I think with Mrs Lloyd it was more to do with security. She felt safe in the knowledge that if she wanted a difficult weed pulled she could call me day or night and I would come out.

It was hard to find two hours' work, but find it I had to because Mrs Lloyd liked to watch me. She tried to be surreptitious about it, but I'd catch her snooping at me from behind the living-room lace. She wasn't doing it for some strange thrill or anything, but simply to check she was getting her money's worth. Now with the cricket season started she had no need to be so voyeuristic. She came out on the terrace, plonked the radio on the table and sat there with her feet up. She just assumed I was a cricket fan; she'd call out the scores and the fall of the wickets. 'Garvaskar caught at silly point again,' she'd report with a laugh. Her hero was Geoffrey Boycott. Whenever he was batting she sat forward and held onto the radio with anxious fingers. She played every shot for him. When he was out she turned the radio off with a slap, said, 'Silly bugger,' and went indoors for a tea interval.

The light of her life was her grandson, four-year-old Leo, who would come to visit with his mother. Most grandmas on the Holly Lodge Estate wanted their grandchildren to be lawyers or doctors, but Mrs Lloyd had other plans. Leo was going to open the batting for his country. That was that. I could always tell when the child was coming to visit because three stumps would be arranged on the lawn, and then as soon as he arrived the bails went on and the session began. Her daughter sat on the terrace and read the newspaper while Mrs Lloyd bowled at the child. I imagined her trying to encourage her daughter in the same way when she had been a little girl and getting no joy. Leo wasn't going to slip through the net, though.

Unfortunately, Leo showed little promise. He would swing and miss, and the ball would go crashing into the flower bed, clean bowling a lupin. I found myself acting as wicketkeeper just to protect the flowers. And Mrs Lloyd didn't hold back. She ran in from the Patio End at pace. Leo would have to face a barrage of short-pitched stuff before he got his drink and biscuit at eleven o'clock. 'Get in line, boy!' she would shout as Leo backed away. 'You're not guarding your off stump.'

After the break Leo would be handed the ball and Mrs Lloyd would bat. 'Pitch it up, child!' she shouted, punishing any delivery that strayed. Mrs Lloyd, normally so proud of her hanging baskets, happily used them as target practice once she had a bat in her hand.

She clipped the ball in my direction once and I caught it. 'Howzat!' both Leo and I appealed.

'Not out,' said a disgruntled Mrs Lloyd.

'Why not?' said Leo.

'He's not a fielder . . . he's the groundsman.'

Gardens all over town became play areas in the heat. If I was to mow a lawn I often had to clear away paddling pools, sun umbrellas or croquet hoops first. Bernie at the garden centre said to me, 'if I sold ice creams here, I'd make a fortune.'

'So why don't you?'

'What?'

'Sell ice creams.'

'I don't know.'

Nugent offered me a glass of lemonade when I visited him. 'I've picked the first of my summer veg,' he said, and proudly presented me with a slug-riddled lettuce.

'In Los Angeles a man shot his neighbour for letting the barbecue smoke blow over the fence,' said Annie Kendal, as she puzzled over the gas-powered, four-wheeled, fan-assisted, twin-burner barbecue 'system' she had just had delivered from Selfridges. The picture on the box was of a happy family sitting at a table, while father, dressed in an apron and chef's hat, served up the chicken drumsticks. That was just how Annie wanted it, but she was struggling. Her toddler could ruin a scene like the one on the box in minutes. He had already decided the most fun you could have with a barbecue was putting the plastic bag that the whole thing came in over your head. Annie dived at him and would have shaken him, but her new-born started to cry upstairs. She looked at me pleadingly and ran inside. I knew that in times like these it was my job to watch little Desmond.

'Look,' I said to him, showing him a clod of earth on my fork, 'a worm.'

He gazed in awe. 'Can I hold it?'

'Course you can.'

I put it in his hand and he put it straight in his mouth.

I went down on one knee. 'Let's not tell your mum about that, OK Desmond?'

Annie put the baby outside in the pram. They'd finally decided to call her Joan. 'What a nice name,' I enthused. Annie shrugged, as if it was simply the name she disliked the least. Anyway, it was too late now. The christening was to be the following weekend, that was what the barbecue was for.

'We're going to have a garden party,' said Annie. 'Lots of family, lots of children.' She looked at me with terror in her eyes. She was dreading the whole idea.

'No, Desmond!' she screamed and I turned to see Desmond sticking a thistle down his throat, like a sword-swallower.

She was in no state to put a barbecue together. So I spent the morning doing it for her, and it put me in such a temper that if one of her neighbours had complained to me about drifting smoke I think I'd have shot him, too.

This ability that other people had to take to their gardens and become vaguely Mediterranean for the period made me envious. I seemed to be doomed to spend my summer evenings in the Black Lion beer garden, which was full of crates, and where the few existing plants were splashed with vomit.

When I got home that evening Neil and I took a bottle of Frascati and some breadsticks down to Mandy's and she put some chairs out on her bare lawn, and we sat there trying to enjoy the summer in this cramped corner of the

109

city. All the garden had was a lilac and a bunch of those yellow jobs that I still didn't know the name of, but which grew everywhere.

Mandy poured another drink and said, 'We could be in Marbella really.'

Neil turned his nose up. 'Bloody insects,' and he picked a fly out of his glass.

'Let's have a game of French cricket,' I suggested.

'How do you play that?' asked Neil.

'You must know how to play French cricket. You just need a bat and a ball.'

None of us had a bat or a ball.

'The English are hopelessly equipped for this sort of weather,' said Neil, blowing his nose.

'We should have a summer party,' said Mandy.

'A barbecue!' I said.

'I hate barbecues,' said Neil.

'You can't hate barbecues,' said Mandy. 'Everyone likes a barbecue.'

'They're messy things. You end up covered in ketchup and pickle and everything is either red raw or carbonised, and you never get a plate and there are never puddings.'

'We can invite friends,' I said.

'I wouldn't like Neil's friends,' said Mandy.

Neil didn't have any friends, just people he'd sold policies to. And girlfriends of course, and they weren't friends really — just names in a phone book.

'I don't know if I'd like your friends either,' said Neil. 'They're all hairdressers.'

'My friends are all sexy and beautiful,' said Mandy, 'and they all have lovely nails.'

We decided to have the party on Saturday night.

*   *   *

Wimbledon progressed into its second week. Chris and Martina were on course to meet in the final. When I went round to Kenneth he had a copy of every newspaper spread out on the kitchen table. He shook his head and said, 'Martina has a ruthlessness I don't like the look of.'

I spent the morning aerating the lawn with a wheeled and spiked device reminiscent of a medieval instrument of torture. 'Look out! It's the aerator!' all the lawn bugs cried, and dived for cover.

Halfway through the morning Kenneth appeared, dressed in cream pleated trousers and a polo shirt. He looked as though he was off to play crown bowls, but he was carrying a box rather the same shape as the one that had contained Annie Kendal's barbecue. A similarly happy family was pictured on the front, but this time, instead of grilling chicken bits, they were playing tennis with plastic racquets and a tennis ball on a length of elastic that was tied to a pole.

Kenneth tackled the instructions systematically, reading them out loud as he went from stage to stage, and eventually he managed to rig the contraption up. Then he took a deep breath and batted the ball for all he was worth. I walked past him a number of times pushing the wheelbarrow, determined not to make eye contact because I knew what he would ask. I ignored his little grunts and exasperations for as long as I could, but then couldn't stop myself glancing over and the whole show looked so pathetic: this fully grown man paddling a ball with a lot of enthusiasm and absolutely no aptitude. He looked as incapable as Rod Laver would have been trying to play Rachmaninov. I had to offer assistance.

'Maybe you need someone at the other end,' I said.

'Oh, would you mind?'

I stood there in my muddy trousers and checked gardening shirt with the frayed collar. Kenneth stood opposite me in his Oxford bags fresh out of the dry cleaners' cellophane. But, now he had an opponent, a steeliness came over him. He said, 'I know, I'll be Chris and you be Martina.'

I winced. I wasn't sure about this at all. '*OK.*'

Then he belted the ball at me as hard as he could. So I belted it back as hard as I could. We slugged it out for twenty minutes. He kept shouting out the score: 15–love, 30–love, 40–love, although he never once explained how he came to be winning all the points. I didn't like to beat him: Martina couldn't beat Chris, not in this garden anyway. Kenneth would have fired me on the spot.

He duly won, and he shook my hand and asked me inside for a cold drink. His Centre Court ticket was pinned to the notice board in the kitchen. He fingered it lovingly. 'She'll win,' he said. 'She always wins when I'm watching.'

Mrs Lloyd was equally primed for the Test Match. She had me mow her lawn to within a centimetre of its life. She wanted a good hard pitch to give her seamers some lift when Leo came the following morning. They would have half an hour's practice in the garden, then off to Lord's.

The match had already started, of course. For the previous two days I'd cycled home past the ground and caught the crowds coming out after a long and hot day's play, and then seen them going in again the following morning as I cycled back up the hill to Hampstead. India had got off to a good start. Mrs Lloyd had sat on the terrace looking more and more concerned as the opening pair piled on the runs.

'It's too good a strip,' she said, and gritted her false teeth. Before I left she had me give the lawn a going-over with the roller.

Across the Heath Annie Kendal was also on edge. The

christening party was heading for meltdown. The barbecue was up, but the paddling pool had sprung a leak. There was a miniature bouncy castle to be inflated, and stacks of plastic chairs to be set out.

'You're expecting a crowd,' I said.

The worst had happened. Everyone she had invited could come. 'If my Uncle Victor drinks too much and meets my husband's brother Harry, you'll read about it in the Sunday papers.'

I gave the hedge a perfunctory clip, then blew up balloons for the rest of the morning. Little Desmond saw me and wanted to play and before I could stop him he was eating earth. Annie yelled at him. Then she ran into the street to yell at some road workers who had started drilling and had woken baby Joan. I left with a smell of burning drifting from the kitchen and Annie yelling, 'Fucking cheese straws!'

Things were much more organised for our garden party at home. I'd even gone round to Lady Brignal's and asked Helen if she'd like to come.

'Can my boyfriend come?'

'Course not.'

'All right then.'

Neil, Mandy and I had each been to the supermarket independently and each come back with about a hundred chipolatas. The fridge looked as though it had some pink creature made of sausage meat living in it.

'At least the party will have a theme,' said Neil.

We bought a lot of cheap beer and a lot of cheap wine and I went to bed and lay with the window wide open, watching next door's gangster cat prowling the street looking for cars to break into. I fell asleep thinking of Kenneth and Wimbledon; of Mrs Lloyd and the Test Match; of Annie Kendal and her christening; of myself and Helen at a party for the first time; and I felt we were all linked in some fateful way.

It started to rain sometime before dawn. I woke with the curtains blowing and an unfamiliar chill in the room. I looked out to see alien black clouds rolling into the city like invading tanks.

It drizzled on and off until ten, when the umpires came out to inspect the pitch at Lords. Then the rain proper came. The covers went back on. There was a little play shortly after lunch – just enough to make sure there wouldn't be a refund – and then it started to pour, and play was abandoned shortly after tea.

Wimbledon suffered the same fate. So did Annie Kendal's christening party, although that didn't feature on *Grandstand*. The rain kept going until the evening, making sure our party was a washout. All Mandy's friends cried off. 'They're frightened of getting their hair wet,' she said. Helen phoned from some distant call box to say the tube station was flooded and all Northern line trains were cancelled and she was going home. The fifteen people who did manage to make it stood out on the lawn under a golf umbrella. Only one of them was female. She was called Parsley and she drank too much of the punch. At midnight she disappeared upstairs with Neil. By two o'clock it was just me and Mandy and a hundred cold sausages. I looked at her and winked and she told me not to be ridiculous and go back to my own flat.

Gardens all over the city wallowed in the rainwater all that night and all the next day. As I cycled to work on Monday the Heath was already growing back its glossy green coat. By Tuesday the heatwave had been forgotten. 'Bloody typical,' said Bernie at the garden centre, standing over his newly arrived fridge from Lyons Maid.

With the cricket finished Mrs Lloyd went back inside and returned to spying on me from various windows. Annie Kendal kept the children indoors – Desmond sat with his nose squashed against the window and watched me work.

When I went to Kenneth's the first thing I heard was the piano playing again, and it was as if the holidays, and the summer, were already over. I didn't like to speak to him about the tennis – Chris had lost to Martina in the end. With the change in the weather it all seemed so long ago.

But when he came out with a drink for me mid-morning he guessed what I wanted to know, and he grinned and said, 'You know the best thing about being an artist?'

'What? Tell me.'

'No matter what you do – books, music, paint – you can be inspired by anything.'

I looked at him blankly.

'It's true, anything that happens to you, good or bad, can be inspiring. For instance, nothing inspires me more than sadness. I came home from the tennis and did some of the best work I've done.' He chuckled. 'Funny, isn't it.'

Then he went indoors and the most haunting music I had ever heard slipped out through the French windows, drawing me towards the house. I peered in and discovered that Kenneth was lying on the couch and the music he was playing was a record, which was a little disappointing, but it didn't deter me: I was able to understand what he meant about gaining strength from adversity, beauty from pain.

As soon as I finished I cycled straight round to Dick and said, 'What's the saddest, most disappointing thing that's ever happened to you?'

He didn't have to think. 'Emma Peel leaving *The Avengers*.'

'Let's write a sketch about it!'

He considered this for a moment then said, 'You know what? I reckon we are taking comedy into unexplored territory.'

'Is that good or bad?'

'It's good . . . I think, although, to be honest, I don't know.'

10

GOLD

Whenever the phone rang at seven in the morning I always knew who it was.

'Gold here,' a voice that had been up for hours would say. 'Got a job for you if you're interested.'

I was always interested in the jobs Mr Gold gave me. They took me all over North London and sometimes beyond, and invariably involved more than just gardening.

And yet the first time I went to his flat I wasn't sure about him at all, largely because he didn't appear to have a garden. He lived in a smart block set back from the Finchley Road, a well-defended fortress with a state-of-the-art intercom system and a layer of the finest double glazing known to man. I rang a bell and a voice told me to take the lift to the third floor. The big electric door buzzed open and then slammed shut behind me like a trap.

What sort of garden does someone have on the third floor, I wondered, as I shared the lift with a woman who glittered with jewellery. She glanced at my muddy knees; I glanced at her ridiculous yellow shoes. We were crossing paths for the first and only time in our lives.

Gold welcomed me into his flat. I offered to take my wellies off, and he put them on a copy of the *Financial Times* by the door. A cat hissed at me as Gold asked me to sit down on a tan leather sofa. 'Let's have some tea,' he said, and went into the kitchen.

Everything in the room had been polished so highly that reflections jumped out and dazzled from every angle: from chandeliers, hearth brasses, picture frames, lustred wood. And despite the traffic on the Finchley Road the room was hushed; it felt immune, a bubble of serenity from which you could gaze down upon the chaotic lives of others who didn't concern you. I was amazed how anyone could achieve such isolation in the middle of London.

Still no sign of a garden, though. Maybe it was a roof job. No, the block was eight floors high. Maybe he wanted someone to water his house plants – maybe he had an indoor marijuana bed growing under infra-red light which he wanted weeding on a regular basis. I'd ask for £2.50 an hour if he did.

Mr Gold returned with a pot of Earl Grey and sat at the other end of the couch. He was sixty years old and wore a fat watch, and didn't look as though he'd done a day's work in his life. The cat jumped on his lap and he stroked it in the style of a James Bond villain. I knew then I had been asked up here for sinister purposes. I was to join the many tradesmen he had lured to his den, people who advertised in shop windows, those no-one would miss. He was about to hypnotise me and ship me off to a place where experiments were carried out on window cleaners, gardeners and decorators.

He passed me a cup of tea and said, 'I own a little house

down in Swiss Cottage. I wonder if you'd like to take a look.'

Gold drove down to Swiss Cottage in his old black car, while I cycled behind. He pulled up outside a three-storey villa that at one time would have housed a well-off family with servants, but had been converted into flats, and was now home to the people that made London tick: the great rented-accommodation crowd. Gold unlocked the gate to an alley which led to a secluded square of garden. The beds were bare; a lonely picnic table stood in the middle of the lawn, its legs lost in the grass; a few buddleia leaned over themselves at breaking point. 'I used to have a man,' said Gold, 'but he left. I believe he took a job mending domestic appliances, washing machines and the like. You can cope with this, I'm sure.'

Sure I could cope with it. Some heavy-duty mowing, some sweat with the pruning saw, some ruthless weeding and job done. Gold wasn't interested in winning prizes, he just wanted his tenants to stop phoning him up and complaining about the jungle outside.

'Good,' said Gold, and he gave me the keys to the tool shed and the gate and told me to come back to his house for my money.

It started to drizzle. I put a hat on and worked until the birds stopped singing, then went and sheltered in the hut. I was watching a spider spin a web from the lawnmower to my elbow when the door to the garden flat opened, and a man stuck his head out and called in an Australian accent, 'You want a drink mate?'

His name was Stu and like his flat he was small and dark – July and he had the lights on in the kitchen. He passed me a tea in a chipped cup with the tea bag still in it, and pushed the packet of sugar my way. This wasn't what I was used to up in Hampstead. Where was my cup and saucer and plate of digestives? This was too much like my house.

Stu was from Melbourne. He'd come over six months ago. 'Australians have to come away for a while,' he said. 'It's a long way.'

He'd worked in bars for most of that time, and he'd travelled round Britain — been to Scotland, stayed with distant relatives in the Midlands. But now he was ready for the big one. 'I've just bought a VW combo,' he said. 'I'm heading off.'

I loved the idea of heading off with a van to sleep in, and all the time in the world. I told him so and he seemed to lap up the reinforcement this gave him. He kept saying, 'You see if you're Australian you have to make the most of a trip like this.' He said it so many times he sounded as though he wasn't convinced, and I began to suspect he was nervous about the whole idea of setting off with everywhere but nowhere to go. He'd turned his dark flat into home. He'd put a few posters up. He had his record player and a little TV. He told me he liked to cook. Everyone was saying to him, 'You have to be an energetic traveller,' but the trouble with Stu was he'd rather have stopped where he was, settled down, got a girlfriend, raised a family. That wasn't what travellers did, though.

'Where are you going to make for?' I asked.

'I'm not sure. All over, you know.'

'When are you going?'

'Oh, any day now.'

He showed me his van parked out on the street. He'd been down to Australia House where there was always a line of VW vans for sale parked outside. 'The trouble is,' he said, 'I don't know much about engines.'

I didn't know much about engines either, but it was clear

this one wasn't going to get him far unless it was all down-hill. The van had a lot of stickers from exotic locations, but nothing about the vehicle encouraged you to believe it had been to any of them. It was no stranger to rust; the bumpers hung at an angle; the tyres looked odd; and when Stu started it up it sounded like a toy.

He didn't seem bothered. He'd driven once round the Aldwych in it and that was good enough for him.

'I was thinking of Africa,' he said. 'Jungle, safari, all that sort of stuff . . .'

'I saw the vehicle half-buried in a sandstorm, vultures circling, and hunched over the wheel the picked-clean skeleton of Stu.

'. . . but then I thought the Far East.'

I saw a monsoon-flooded field and there in the middle was the van with the door slapping in the gale and Stu's wrinkled body slumped in the cab.

'But I've always wanted to head north, so maybe I'll head to Norway and the North Cap.'

I saw the top of the vehicle just visible in a snowdrift and, inside, a perfectly preserved frozen corpse. And when I looked at Stu I knew that was what he saw as well. But what could he do? He couldn't go back home until he'd had the big over-land adventure. Everyone would laugh at him otherwise.

Now he was looking at me helplessly. 'Where do you think I should go?'

'Hampshire's nice.'

The rain stopped. I went back outside and started digging over the beds. But soon Stu was there next to me. He had this habit of standing with his hands in his pockets looking up at the ceiling or the sky, and screwing up his nose as if he'd spotted a leaking pipe, or a rare bird. It made me look up too. Nothing there.

He said, 'I'm glad he's got a gardener. It could do with a few flowers, this place. Bit of colour.'

I told him I didn't think Mr Gold would stretch to flowers, grass was his limit.

'Few flowers, bit of garden furniture. It would be nice to sit out here and have lunch, that sort of thing.'

Stu didn't really listen.

I asked him, 'You came over here on your own?'

'It's the only way to travel,' he replied. But then added, 'I was going to come with a friend, but he pulled out.'

So it wasn't the only way to travel at all. He looked back at the sky again. I think what Stu would have liked was someone to push him into leaving. Or, better still, someone to go with him. A terrible thought entered my head. I looked at Stu and I knew what he was going to say next.

'Tell you what. You could come with me.'

Dave Allen didn't go for the boxer and the Pope sketch. 'Keep trying,' wrote the script editor. 'Remember, Dave's humour comes from the world around us.'

Dick said, 'That's it! We're sitting indoors trying to write when we should be out experiencing the world around us. It's obvious!'

So we went for a walk along the canal towpath, the back-yard of London from Hackney up to Little Venice. We passed drunks, canoeists, cyclists, lovers and one woman sitting on a bench cross-legged, chanting. Not one sketch for Dave Allen suggested itself, though. I asked Dick, 'What would you say if I said I was thinking of going on an overland trip to Africa, or somewhere, in a VW van with an Australian named Stu?'

'I'd say, is there a sketch in it?'

'I don't think there is.'

'Then why are you doing it?'

'There are other things in life beside comedy sketches.'

Dick looked serious. 'But nothing more important . . . Anyway, you can't stop now. Success is just round the corner.'

We turned a corner and Dick stopped. 'What's that?' He was pointing to a pile of construction material, slabs and girders for repairs to the canal. But beneath it all was what looked like part of the body of a snake. That was odd enough, but the way the snake was laced through the slabs it must have been eight foot long. Then we realised we were right by London Zoo.

We hurried to the zoological offices and managed to grab a research assistant who was clearly unhappy at the idea of snakes altogether, but said he'd come and see. He went off to find some snake-catching equipment, and came back with a bucket and a mop.

We led him back to the towpath. The snake was still there, our credibility was intact. The research assistant squinted at it, checked one end then checked the other, and said, 'Grass snake.'

'Grass snake! It's eight foot long.'

'Grass snake,' said the research assistant, and put his mop back in his bucket.

It was a cover-up – it had to be. The public panic would have been too great had the truth about an escaped python got out. But we couldn't argue. What we could do was write a sketch about a zoo where the animals are planning a breakout, digging a tunnel, an exotic species' retelling of *The Great Escape*. 'See,' said Dick. 'That's the best sketch we've ever written, and you were thinking of running off to Africa.'

I wondered if it was the right sort of material for Dave Allen.

'He'll love it,' said Dick. 'He can play the camel.'

* * *

I said to Mandy downstairs, 'If you could go anywhere and have the time of your life, where would it be?'

'John Lewis,' she said.

'The only place worth going to is India,' said Neil. 'It's the home of spiritual fulfilment and there's a budding home insurance industry.'

I suggested India to Stu but he said, 'I've got a sensitive stomach.'

'How about a circumnavigation of the Black Sea?'

'You know what we really need in this garden?' he said. 'A bird table.'

He presented me with a few trays of annuals he had bought. 'I thought we could plant them,' he said to me.

'You're leaving any day!' I had a note of panic in my voice, as if I was the one with a train to catch.

'. . . brighten the place up a bit,' he went on, ignoring me.

We planted them – petunias and pansies, and some seed packets of nasturtium.

'They'll take a month to come up,' I said.

But he wasn't bothered. He just looked at the sky and said, 'The more I live in this flat the nicer it gets. What's a nice climbing plant for that fence?'

'Clematis,' I said. 'Why?'

'No reason.'

Next time I went round, there was a honeysuckle planted at one end of the fence and a clematis at the other.

'Come and have a look at the van,' he said. 'I've been working on it, getting her ready for the big off.'

He had been working on it, but not on the engine or the brakes or anything important. He'd put new curtains up, and cleaned the cooker. The exhaust was falling off but he had spent his time patching the carpet. I said to him, 'Stu, something about this whole venture seems flawed to me.'

He nodded. 'Have you thought about coming?'

'I can't come.'

'Why not?'

'I . . . just can't.'

'Why not?'

'Because of Dave Allen.'

'The comedian with the finger missing?'

'Yes.'

Not surprisingly, he didn't know why that was stopping me. Surprisingly, he didn't bother to ask. He just frowned slightly, and said, 'We get him in Australia.'

There was another reason why I couldn't go. I knew that the day after I left, Helen would finish with her boyfriend and wonder where I was when she needed me. I told her my dilemma, that I was tempted to pack it all in and head off, hoping I might detect a hint of regret in her response, but she said, 'You should go!'

'You think so?'

'You don't get chances like this very often.'

'I don't know.'

'I mean there's absolutely nothing to stop you, is there?'

She suggested all Stu needed was someone to organise him. So she came with me to Swiss Cottage Library and we pulled out atlases and maps, and plotted wonderful journeys across the wildest parts of the world. 'How about Trans-Sahara,' she said, in the manner of a travel agent. 'You cross the desert through the Empty Quarter to Tamanrasett. There you spend time with the Tuareg, experiencing first-hand their ancient and fascinating ways. From there you travel on to Timbuktu, and have your picture taken by the Welcome To road sign. Then you proceed downriver by steamboat to Mali. From there it's overland through the rainforest to Senegal.'

Not bad, but I countered with a journey through the frozen north. 'You set out from Euston station on the sleeper to Edinburgh, then on to Thurso where you take the boat to the Orkneys, on to Shetlands, and then the Faroes. From the Faroes it's a skip and a jump to Iceland, then round the coast of Greenland by ferry-hop, finally hitchhiking a ride on a fishing boat to Newfoundland, from where you take a bus down through the Maritimes to New York, ending your journey with a night in the Waldorf-Astoria.'

This was great fun. It was also good for our geography. I had never heard of Baluchistan before, but now I was familiar with its bank holidays and railway timetable.

After the library closed we found ourselves wandering through Belsize Park testing each other on capital cities. It was a warm evening and when a bus passed heading towards Highgate I had an irresistible idea.

'Do you want to hear some live music?'

Before she could answer I had pushed her on the bus and we headed up the hill. We jumped off by Highgate School and walked down to the playing fields and nipped over the fence.

'Where are you taking me?'

We were going to Kenneth's house.

I found his gate and slipped into his back garden. If I'd asked to sit on his lawn of an evening and listen while he played I'm sure he would have let me, but I was enjoying leading Helen through the dark.

Sure enough, Kenneth was playing the piano. We crept along trying not to crack twigs, and crouched by the shed. The French doors to the house were closed and it wasn't always easy to hear the music, but Helen was holding her breath with excitement. 'What tune is that?' she whispered.

'Schubert,' I said, knowing that it had been written the

day before for the biscuit commercial Kenneth was working on.

'It's beautiful,' she said, and we sat there in silence with the occasional bat darting across the lawn, and I felt happy and proud because I knew neither of us would ever forget this evening.

The house in Swiss Cottage wasn't Mr Gold's only property by any means. He owned houses all over London: big flats, little flats, flats in Kensington, flats in Hackney. I wondered where he got his money from; he didn't seem like someone who had spent his life dealing on the property market. He was more interested in things artistic. I would go round to his flat at the end of each week and pick up my wages and he'd always invite me in for a cup of Earl Grey and ask me what I thought of the picture he'd just snapped up. I'd look at it with a suitably pained expression, and say something strange like, 'It reminds me of two planets colliding,' in the hope he might think I was enigmatic and give me a raise.

When it was time to leave he'd pull a brown envelope out of his back pocket and say, 'You'd better count it.' The notes were always new. You couldn't imagine Mr Gold handling used money.

I liked working for him because whenever he phoned it was as if I was being given a mission. He'd hand me an address and just say, 'You'll know what's got to be done.'

One morning he asked me to go round to a house in Holloway. 'The garden needs reclaiming,' he said. 'I've got some tree surgeons there. You'll have to work around them.'

There was hardly a garden there at all. The plot was void of life because the trees that overhung it had blocked out all light for years. The tree surgeons arrived, although surgeon was rather a grand title for these guys. One man had a shaved head and clutched a chainsaw as if it was a machine gun. He introduced himself as Murphy. His assistant was a pale and skinny lad who didn't seem to want to get out of the pickup.

I worked steadily, redefining beds, pruning back the buddleia again – buddleia seemed to be the only thing that ever grew in Gold's gardens. Meanwhile, above me, the tree surgeons were having problems. Murphy was shouting at his sidekick, 'What do you mean you suffer from vertigo?'

The lad had come from the agency. He'd been hired for the day. He'd just been told it was manual work. 'No-one said anything about climbing trees.'

'You've got to climb the bloody tree,' said Murphy. 'It's part of being a tree surgeon.'

The forceful approach wasn't going to work, though. The lad had to sit down; just the sight of the ladder upset him. He saw me watching and looked at me, pleadingly. 'I'm a history student.' He'd only wanted a holiday job; he hadn't wanted to face his worst fear.

Murphy, to his credit, let his sensitive side surface. 'A tree surgeon scared of heights? It's a funny old world.'

Not as funny as all that, it turned out. Before I could say no, Murphy had persuaded me to take the history student's place. 'It's not difficult,' he said. 'You just have to sit in the tree and do what I say.'

So I spent the rest of the day in a tree, while the history student happily did my gardening. My job was to tie ropes onto the branches that Murphy was cutting, and hold onto them so they wouldn't fall onto neighbouring roofs. It didn't take long to realise that this was about as much fun as one could have as a gardener. Not because the work was thrilling or it was good to work with trees or anything like that, but because, suspended thirty feet up in a dense urban area, you have a view into every window in the neighbourhood.

A man playing chess with himself was the first thing I saw. He sat back, scratched his head, then leaned forward and made a move. Then he went and sat on the opposite chair, leaned back, scratched his head, made another move and returned to his original seat.

In another room a woman stood ironing a pair of underpants the size of a hot-air balloon. Her child saw me watching and aimed his bow and arrow at me. A bang made me turn and there was a man with a hammer fashioning some sort of metalwork sculpture on his fire escape.

Every branch that Murphy lopped off would reveal a new view: a woman grooming her poodle, a man playing air guitar to Led Zeppelin; the weatherman on the TV; a girl in dungarees practising scales on her clarinet.

I was in a crow's-nest looking down on this sea of people. A young woman came into her flat, kicked off her shoes, took her jacket off, let her hair down and walked into the bedroom . . . A church clock struck five. 'We'll call it a day,' said Murphy.

'Hang on, just a minute!' I pleaded. But he was down the tree faster than I'd seen him do anything all day, and dragging me down with him.

Back at Stu's flat, it was all activity. Not in preparation for his trip, of course. The action was in the garden, where I found him planting an apple tree.

'Have you throught of Morocco?' I said.

'Don't think so.'

'The road to Damascus?'

'Don't fancy it.'

Even Mr Gold, who hated to lose a tenant, became excited

when he heard Stu was embarking on the journey of a life-time. 'Zanzibar,' he said. 'I know a very nice hotel there where you can get *anything* you want.' Mr Gold was becoming more and more mysterious.

But Stu just grinned when you talked about his journey, and tried to bring the conversation back to the garden. He spent an afternoon rummaging through the rubble I'd dug out of the beds. He wheelbarrowed out the bits he needed and arranged them into a rockery. I said to him, 'This is the garden with everything.'

'Not quite,' he said. 'It needs one more thing – a pond.'

'A pond?'

'No garden is complete without a pond.'

The pond he dug that week was small but beautifully crafted. He buried a kidney-shaped fibreglass mould in front of the new rockery, then he put in marsh marigolds and lilies. 'I wanted a fountain,' he said. 'But Mr Gold won't allow the plumbing.'

So he put goldfish in instead. I took him to Bernie's garden centre. Bernie wanted to sell him goldfish by the pound, like a fishmonger, but Stu was much more selective. He chose three chubby ones. 'Want an ice cream with that?' Bernie asked.

Stu named the fish after Australian mountain ranges: Bluey, Snowy and Flinders. He poured them into the pond. And that was that. There was nothing else to do. He opened two beers and we sat down at the picnic table as the sun set behind the building and cast the garden into six o'clock shade.

'We've created something here,' he said. And he was right, the garden was an achievement. He had turned this little corner of Swiss Cottage from a dump into a haven. It was a tribute to what someone can do when he doesn't want to do something else.

With his beer finished and the sun gone down he could procrastinate no longer. He'd spent the past three weeks looking at the ground but now he was back gazing at the sky again. He was like a migratory bird, leaving it until the last possible minute. But when I looked at him now I could sense he was ready. He asked, 'Sure you don't want to change your mind and come along?'

That night I lay awake, trying not to recognise a life-changing moment when it was staring me in the face. I could jump out of bed, pack a bag, leave Neil a note and go round to Stu's place and this time tomorrow be motoring into the Alps heading for wherever.

I lay listening to the radio and every song was telling me to go, and I was going to go, I really was, but . . . suddenly it was morning, and I knew it was too late.

I cycled as fast as I could round to Stu's flat. The van was gone and so was he. Only Gold was there, doing an inventory on the flat. He said Stu had put an envelope through his door with the rent that was due, and a note attached to it. He had decided on the big one. He was going to drive home to Australia.

And over the next few weeks postcards arrived. But they weren't from Paris or Amsterdam, the places he'd said he wanted to visit. They were from industrial towns in Germany and obscure villages in Yugoslavia. They were all accounts of the garages he had been towed to, and of the towns he had had to stay in while he waited for parts. I wanted the cards to be full of the joys of being on the road, of the people he had met, of some sort of self-discovery, but he reported on the prices in supermarkets and garden centres. He didn't seem to be enjoying himself.

He always asked about the garden, whether the clematis

had bloomed, and had I remembered to pinch out the tips of the dahlias when they started to grow. He always asked if there had been rain. I couldn't answer him, of course — he gave no address. But that was fortunate. The garden he had created was high maintenance. It needed someone to water it daily; it needed the person who lived in the garden flat to take care of it. I did it for a while, but then there was a hot spell and the hanging baskets began to wilt. The greenfly got to work. One morning I looked in the pond and the goldfish were gone. A Spanish woman living on the second floor called out to me, 'Ducks! The ducks they eat them,' and she flapped her arms like wings and did a very good imitation of a duck diving into a pond and coming up with a fish.

A man from Nottingham took over the garden flat. He laughed at the idea of looking after the garden. He was doing up a property to move into, he said; he wouldn't be here long. The flowers faded; the weeds took over; only the old perennials survived.

Another card came from Greece, then one from a town not far from Istanbul. Then silence, and I never heard from Stu again.

11

ROBERTSON, DORM-SKORY AND WALTERS

Gardening, the great British obsession, the window on the nation. Like cars and dogs, gardens told the truth about their owners. From the overstocked, much mulched, well-watered ornamental showpiece, to the concrete patch of weeds and cardboard boxes out the back, gardens never lied.

'That's a very interesting theory,' said Bernie at the garden centre, during one of our many discussions on gardening and the psychosociological state of the nation. 'I've always been of the opinion that humans have an inbuilt need to garden. If gardening hadn't existed we would have had to invent it.'

'We did invent it.'

'Exactly.'

It was the season when gardens and gardeners were at their most conspicuous, and nowhere could their behaviour be better observed than the cul-de-sac where I had managed to get three jobs in three different houses. They were all next-door neighbours and their facades of lace and pebbledash presented a united and formidable defence, but their back gardens told very different stories, and the fences that separated them were like cultural divides.

Mrs Robertson was the first to employ me. She was a woman of charm and warmth when I knocked on her front door, all smiles and a giggly hello. But when she saw my wellington boots and realised who I was, she instructed me to go round to the back.

And there, she was a lot more brisk: her smile was pursed, her greeting businesslike. She even had the nerve to interview me. She sat me down at her dining-room table and fired questions at me – none of them to do with gardening. 'Have you ever been in prison?'

'No.'

'What would you do if you found a purse in the street?'

'Give it to a policeman.'

'Can you change a plug?'

'Yes.'

'What river runs through Budapest?'

'The Danube?'

I got the job.

Mrs Robertson knew exactly what she wanted out of her garden, she wanted a natural habitat. She wanted nothing to do with plants she labelled pompous, like hibiscus and fuchsia. She stuck her nose in the air and said, 'I'm not a city person. I grew up in Worcester. It was all fields and animals when I was a child; and apples that tasted of apples. I want to revel in nature.'

She hadn't lived in London long. She'd come here to make some money and run, and she was going to be ruthless. She took me round the garden wearing a blue trouser suit. I noticed her shoes matched her make-up. She made it clear she held the neighbourhood, indeed the whole city, in contempt – she was doing London a favour by living here. She laughed and said, 'I won't be here long.' I got the impression she wanted to impress upon me that she was impressive.

She said she hated the way Londoners tried to tame their greenery. 'Too many people in the city want to turn their gardens into showcases,' she said. 'As if they have something to prove.' And I thought: she's trying to prove to me she has nothing to prove.

'I hate ornamental gardens,' she sighed. 'All those hybrid flowers and crazy paving.'

'Oh I agree,' I said, and immediately thought: hang on, I'm talking myself out of a job here. A showcase of nature was all very well, but it basically required me not to do anything, to just let nature get on it. What did she want me to do: turn up once a week and not cut the grass, then not bother with the deadheading?

For all her talk, however, Mrs Robertson was suspect. 'Think wild,' she kept saying to me, 'think freedom!' but she wanted every corner of her natural paradise to have a job description, whether it was to attract bumblebees, or be a service station for migratory birds, or a haven for wild flowers. Whenever I arrived she slipped into site fore-person mode and talked about targets and performance goals. She would stand in the middle of the lawn and say things like, 'The success of any project depends on sound planning.' Then she'd look at her watch and march inside with a 'I've got to call America.' Mrs Robertson wanted a wilderness all right, but she wanted it on her own terms.

Two doors down from her lived Dr Dormskory. He caught me as I was leaving one morning and asked me if I would do a weekly session for him as well. He was a doctor of physics, a man in his sixties who wore a hat indoors and had an accent that made him sound like a Soviet spy. He rolled his own cigarettes in a little machine, and spent most of his time working in his study upstairs which looked over the garden. His desk was at the window and I could see the top of his hat as he worked, searching for a solution that would make the world a better place for all nations.

In contrast to Mrs Robertson all Dr Dormskory wanted was a peaceful life, calm and order. He wanted no surprises. Every plant in his garden was a different shade of green, even the flowers had green blooms. He didn't want to come out one morning and find something bright pink. Green kept him soothed.

But this quest for serenity would always be hard for a man like the doctor. He was a tortured genius, who wore his insecurity on his sleeveless pullover. He said he wanted the garden to relax in, but whenever he came out he sat hunched in a knot of tension. I caught him tearing a leaf into little pieces once. In an attempt to calm him I asked him what he was working on, and he looked up at me and hissed, 'Nature is so damned perfect.' And then he sighed hopelessly, hauled himself to his feet and wandered back inside.

He couldn't cope with anything that was half right, anything that could be interpreted. He wanted precision or nothing at all. His brow was destined to be forever furrowed, his fingers forever yellowed from the cigarettes that he lifted to his mouth with a tremor. He wanted to see things in straight lines, but I suspected that the carpet in his room was worn in a circle of frustration, and the piece of paper on his desk was permanently blank. He was looking for a universal truth, but it was killing him.

When the mood took him he liked to come into the garden and rearrange things. I'd spend the whole morning digging up plants, shrubs, trees and then replanting them in different positions according to his whim. I found his indecisiveness catching. 'When are you coming next week?' he'd ask.

'Monday,' I'd say.

'Are you sure?'

'Maybe Wednesday.'

'Either day suits me. So does Friday.'

'I'll come Tuesday.'

'Fine. Morning or afternoon?'

'Not sure.'

I saw him on the Heath once. Head down, hands in pockets, his feet moving in a shuffle. I said hello and he looked up and nodded, but I knew he hadn't recognised me.

When I met his wife one morning as she was leaving for work, she shook my hand and said quietly, 'Is he giving you any trouble?'

'No.'

'He's got so much on his mind.'

One day he seemed particularly on edge. He paced round and round his room, then paced up and down the garden. Then he sat on the bench and put his head in his hands. He seemed to be wrestling with something huge. Suddenly he jumped to his feet. I expected him to say 'Eureka!' But instead he said, 'I want to move this bench.'

I didn't like the sound of this. I said, 'Fine. Where to?'

He started to sweat. It was a huge question for a man of Dr Dormskory's intellect. The trouble with a bench was there were just too many places it could go, and if you put it in one place it meant it couldn't go in any of the others.

He laboured with the problem for a long time. We tried the bench on the lawn, the patio, the middle of the rockery. Just where did a bench belong in the space–time continuum? Then he stopped, looked at me and smiled. 'Of course.' And he marched indoors.

'What about the bench?' I called.

'What?'

'The bench, where do you want it?'

'Oh, put it back where it was.'

Next thing I saw him in his room, head down, working away. The problem solved, the world saved, for now.

In between Dr Dormskory and Mrs Robertson lived the Walters, and it was when they asked me to come to them and complete the chain that this little enclave began to present itself as worthy of study.

Of all the three, Mr Walters was the most dangerous. He was a thin man with long fingers, married to a woman who reminded me of a nicely coiffured poodle. She stood obediently at his side and yet he always spoke of her as if she wasn't there. 'Mrs Walters likes her herbaceous border well defined,' he said. 'She likes her flowers in rows, six inches apart, in descending order of height.' He wanted to be thought of as a reasonable, well-organised man, but it didn't take me long to realise his garden was a monument to fascism. He liked strong colours, roses and dahlias, and he liked to walk the length of his beds, inspecting his upright rows of marigolds as if he was a visiting head of state. But unlike Major Chesney, whose military stiffness had something of the Home Guard about it, there was the air of a dictator about Walters. He ruled with an iron glove. Any plant not pulling its weight, anything stunted or not colourful enough, he demanded I dig up and commit to the compost. Any plants threatening to invade another's territory were swiftly extracted and burned. Mr Walters believed strongly in nipping in the bud.

He was obsessive over his privacy. Screen was his favourite word, and gardening for him was really little more than assisting him in his quest to keep the rest of the world at bay. One day he asked me to help him extend his fence. I could see no gaps in it, but then I realised he didn't want it longer, he wanted it higher. Most of the shrubs he planted weren't chosen for their foliage or scent, but for their potential as blockades. He moaned when aeroplanes flew over his space. 'They give Mrs Walters a headache,' he said. And of course he moaned about his neighbours. Dr Dormskory was a communist. 'He's got plants in that garden that don't belong in this country.' Mrs Robertson was a feminist. 'Never see her in a skirt.' He moaned about the council. He moaned about the weather. And what about the price of petrol? And as for the cost of sending a letter to Canada!

When I wasn't stopping things coming into Walters's garden I was killing things that had somehow got past the defences. Each session would start with spraying the roses, or putting down slug pellets. Weeds were genetically cleansed. Fungus didn't stand a chance. Cankers were cut out with glee. Victims of blight were ceremoniously burnt at sunset.

And while every tool he owned was ancient and held together with tape, his arsenal of pest-killers was on the cutting edge of extermination technology. His shed had a whole shelf dedicated to pesticides. Weeds were zapped with Weed-a-Kill, moss exterminated with Moss-Gone, cats kept at bay with Cat-Shoo. Once I lifted a paving stone and found an army of ants following a well-worn path. Walters was appalled. 'Mrs Walters can't abide ants,' he said, and marched off to arm himself.

I expected him to come back with a kettle of boiling water, but that was too good for them. He lit a blowtorch and incinerated the whole colony. Then he dumped a pound of Ant-Away powder on the nest for good measure. It was chemical warfare. He pretended he didn't enjoy any of this, but I never saw him happier than the morning he put on a protective suit and mask and sprayed an apple tree.

His creation of Little England was capped by his collection of windmills and gnomes and miniature cottages that he had dotted around. He had model birds in the trees — which I suspect he preferred to the real things — and he had a little stream pumped from his pond in a loop round the bottom of the rockery. Over the stream was a bridge on which stood a wooden couple who gazed over the idyll that surrounded them. I saw them as models of Walters and his wife, living in the perfect world they had created for themselves in their back garden where everything worked, and there was no crime, no dog crap on the pavement, and there was no interference from the French or indeed the rest of the human race.

Then one morning I found him in a state. He was staring at his lawn as if something terrible had happened in the night, as if one of the gnomes had been sexually assaulted or his little pagoda sprayed with graffiti. But no, his garden had been invaded by a force he had not encountered before. In the middle of the lawn, standing proud like an enemy fortress, was a molehill, fresh and brown and perfectly formed.

'How about that!' I said, quite thrilled at the idea. I hadn't seen molehills in Hampstead before. 'Of all the gardens he could choose he chose yours.'

'Bastard,' muttered Walters. 'Little bastard!' And he had a maniacal look in his eye, a look that all the poisons of

Fisons could not have washed clean. Rather than welcome this little visitor he was preparing himself for battle.

'Right,' said Walters, trying to hide his excitement, 'I need the correct equipment.' And he got in his car and free-wheeled down the hill to the shops. It seemed his arsenal of poisons and pesticides wasn't comprehensive enough to cope with a mole; he wanted reinforcements. He didn't want the mole to know what had hit it.

I wondered if he was going to come back with some mole-catching animal, like a polecat or something, but he returned with smoke pellets. 'See how the little bugger likes these!' he said, digging into the hill and locating the tunnel. He lit the fuse and bunged the canister in. 'Back,' he said, as if he had just thrown a grenade into a bunker.

It turned out that the 'little bugger' liked smoke just fine. Next time I called there were two more molehills, and Walters was gnashing his teeth. 'Look at the bags under his eyes,' said Mrs Walters. She told me she had woken at five o'clock that morning and found him gone from his bed. She'd lifted the curtain and seen him creeping across the lawn in his slippers and dressing gown, a garden fork raised above his head, waiting to pounce the moment the mole-hill as much as trembled. After an hour he'd come in empty-handed, and refused breakfast.

He had tried petrol-soaked rags; he'd tried mothballs; he'd tried broken glass down the hole. Now he paced the garden like Rommel, endeavouring to work out the mentality of his adversary. The suburban bliss he had spent years creating wasn't going to be undone in a few days by a pink-nosed, myopic rodent who didn't know his place.

'Cup of tea, dear?' said Mrs Walters, trying to ease him.

Walters looked at her as if she was mad, and said one word: 'Garlic.'

Garlic was his last chance. Garlic down the hole would get rid of the illegal immigrant. I felt like pointing out that garlic was for vampires, but nothing would change Walters's mind once he had decided on a strategy. Mrs Walters produced a bulb of garlic as ordered, and Walters broke it up into cloves and stuffed it down the tunnel. 'It's an old wives' tale,' he admitted to me. 'I never thought I would have to resort to this.'

I tried to help by asking other clients how they dealt with moles.

'You don't get many round here,' said Nugent. 'But the best thing to get rid of them is human urine.' I should have guessed he'd say that. As I should have guessed what Mrs Lavenham's reaction would be. 'Put a saucer of milk out for them every night.'

Bernie's response was:

'"A weed is no more than a flower in disguise, Which is seen through at once, if love give a man eyes."'

'What?'

'James Lowell, 1848.'

He was reading from a book of gardening quotes he had just put out for sale. 'Got something witty to say about every aspect of gardening. It's the perfect gift.'

'What does it say about moles?'

He flicked through the book. 'Moles: "Your worst enemy becomes your best friend, once he's underground." Euripides.'

'I don't get it.'

'I don't get it either.'

It didn't matter, the next time I went round to see Walters he was jubilant. It seemed as if garlic had done the trick. He sat on the terrace with a can of shandy. 'Haven't had a peep out of the blighter since.' How he laughed. In fact he laughed rather more than he should have done. Later I discovered why. The mole had simply decamped to next door.

Dr Dormskory's attitude was altogether different. 'I've got a mole,' he said to me, and appeared to be confused by the very idea.

'Lucky you,' I said. I was still on the mole's side; surely it would be welcome here?

'No no no,' said the doctor. 'It can't stay here.'

'Why not?'

This stumped him. 'I'll tell you later,' he said, and put his jacket on and went out.

He had left me a list of things to do. Top of the list was to replant some ferns in two equal rows on opposing sides of the garden. The word equal was underlined so many times the pencil had worn through the paper. But this wasn't unusual for Dormskory. Above all he wanted his garden to be symmetrical. If you clipped the hedge on one side you had to clip it to the exact same height on the other. A hebe planted on one corner had to have one at the opposite diagonal. A morning working for him was 50 per cent gardening, 50 per cent geometry.

He returned two hours later with a pile of library books. 'I've been reading about moles,' he said. 'Did you know they have to eat their own body weight every three days?'

'I didn't.'

'They can also move their own body weight in earth every minute. They live almost their entire life underground, only coming to earth to collect leaves for a nest.'

'Remarkable.'

'They are very interesting little mammals indeed.'

'Good.'

'And there are some very interesting ways to get rid of them!'

I didn't like the sound of this. Any solution that Dormskory thought of would be precise and final and maybe even nuclear. He produced a bottle and said, 'What you need to do is cut off their . . .'

'Their what?'

'Their food supply.'

He handed me the bottle. 'Castor oil.'

'Castor oil?'

'They don't like it. You need to saturate the lawn with it. It'll do the trick.'

I did exactly what he told me. For the rest of the morning I watered the lawn with a 50–1 solution of castor oil and water.

And the mole went next door to Mrs Robertson.

But this was good news, surely. Mrs Robertson wanted a natural garden and you couldn't get more natural than a mole.

'You've got a mole!' I said with glee.

'I know that,' she said, without glee.

'It's a privilege. You don't get many round here. This is good news.'

She tried to look pleased. But she had the kind of smile I suspected she reserved for people she was about to deal with in some horrible way. The phone went and she strode indoors.

I spent the morning trying to mess the garden up, as I normally did, trying to make sure nothing looked too culti-vated. I was distracted, though. I found myself identifying with the mole. I wanted to give it a name. I wondered if I should suggest to Mrs Robertson she leave a saucer of milk out. I wondered if she wanted to stay up with me one night and mole-watch.

'"Your worst enemy becomes your best friend, once he's underground,"' I said to her before I left.

'I beg your pardon.'

'Euripides.'

At home I too read up on moles. I discovered they had appalling eyesight but remarkable hearing. No mole had ever been domesticated. I began to wonder if there was a way to encourage moles into your garden instead of deterring them. I said to Mandy downstairs, 'Wouldn't you like a mole?'

'No! Moles, warts, I hate them.'

I dreamed of the day when it was a mark of status among gardeners to have molehills in your garden; when the mole became the symbol of the National Trust; the day when Bernie stocked false molehills in his garden centre; the day when the mole, like the red squirrel, had a preservation order slapped on it.

It was just a dream. Next time I went round to Mrs Robertson the mole's lifeless body was lying on the patio. She was displaying it like a trophy. 'I caught it in a trap,' she said. And when she saw my disappointment, she added, 'This is what we do in the country. We don't get sentimental over animals. It's survival of the fittest.'

I had to control myself. Life to her seemed to be all about stamping on the person, or mole, beneath you. I wanted to hit her with the rake. The mole population just needed a good leader, someone to inspire the moles of the South-east, and they would gather together and gang up on people like Mrs Robertson, and teach her where she really stood in the food chain.

After this, I couldn't take her talk of a wilderness seriously.

I think she began to realise she was only fooling herself as well. She started to ask me to tidy things up and clear the nettles out, until one day she said to me, 'I'm thinking of putting bark chippings down on the beds – organic ones, of course,' and I knew the kind of self-delusional person she really was. She'd be installing cheap garden furniture from the Indonesian rainforest before the summer was out.

'There's a quote in here that sums her up,' Bernie said, waving his little book at me. 'You want to hear it?'

'Go on then.'

'"When a man says to me, 'I have the intensest love of nature,' at once I know that he has none." There. A bloke called Emerson said that, in his journals, 1857.'

12

DR AND MRS GLOVER

Jobs came and went. Some people wanted to employ me for a single morning, others would need me until the day they died.

As the summer set in I seemed to have a never-ending supply of work, so much that I stopped advertising. I felt in control of this gardening business. I began to think there was little that clients could throw at me that I couldn't cope with. But I had grown complacent. When I went to work for Dr and Mrs Glover I found myself in a situation where I was helpless. It was the only job from which I was ever sacked.

Most of my work still came by word of mouth, or perhaps someone would see me digging in a front garden and ask me if I'd like to call on them. The job at the Glovers was unusual from the start because it came to me courtesy of a wasp sting.

I was cycling down a hill when the wasp collided with me, bounced off my chin and dipped down my shirt. I whacked my chest a few times. Cars swerved to avoid me as I cycled along at a wobble. But my attack on the wasp only managed to annoy it more and it stung me on my upper arm.

'Put some butter on it,' said Mandy. 'My mother always put butter on wasp stings.'

We had no butter so I put sunflower spread on it. By the next morning my arm had swollen up like one of Popeye's. It was tight and red and the swelling showed no sign of reducing. I cycled off to work, but even the effort of pedalling was making my arm throb painfully. I decided I needed medical help so I chained my bike to the railings of the Royal Free Hospital and went into casualty.

'I've been stung by a wasp,' I said to the receptionist.

'Where?' she enquired without looking up.

'Coming down Highgate Hill.'

She raised her head, slowly, and gave a tired sigh – didn't I know this was casualty? The only jokes permitted came from the staff.

'On my arm,' I said, and rolled up my sleeve for her.

She waved me to the waiting area. I took my place among a variety of workers: carpenters, plumbers, roofers, with bandaged hands, heads or feet. It looked like the tradesmen's entrance of casualty. In a different ward with a nice carpet were the solicitors and company directors who waited with much more respectable injuries.

I was duly called and led to a tiny cubicle with a tiny bed, where a big doctor examined me. His nametag said Dr Glover. He pulled out a syringe and tried to make conversation. 'What do you do for a living?'

'I'm a gardener.'

'Really.' All eyes were on the needle as he bled it and turned to me. 'You're probably very busy at the moment, middle of summer.'

'Yes . . .'

'Shame. We could do with a gardener. Don't suppose you've got time to come round and have a look.'

There are few certainties in life, but one of them is that you will do your utmost to keep a man happy if he is holding a hypodermic needle over you. 'Sure,' I said.

'When could you come?'

'Oh any time.'

'How about tomorrow?'

'Fine.'

'Jolly good,' and he gave me a hospital smile as he gently slid the needle into me.

The next day I turned up at the good doctor's house in Gospel Oak. He wouldn't be in, he had said, but his wife would see to me. The doctor was a man in his late fifties, with fat fingers, and chest hair poking out from under his collar. I expected his wife to be a corresponding female, someone with sensible shoes and hair set once a month by Raymond. But Mrs Glover was a complete surprise. She was younger and not only more beautiful than her husband, but also more handsome. She was on the verge of middle age, but didn't look as if she was going to slip into it without a fight. She had glossy lips and painted toenails, and she pulled open the front door with a girly 'hi'. She was like a housewife from a mail-order catalogue.

'You're the gardener, aren't you?' she said, before I could speak. 'My husband told me all about you.'

She led me through the house, through the kitchen and sun-lounge extension. The house mirrored her perfectly. All smooth edges, and soft furnishings, all yellows and creams, comfort and joy. 'How's your arm?' she said.

'Fine, thank you. Your husband's a pretty good doctor.'

'Coffee?'

That was what the house smelt of, fresh coffee. She had a pot on a warmer, and a collection of mugs nearby, each with a slogan on it. She filled one and handed it to me. It read: Greetings from Aberdeen.

When we went outside she put sunglasses on and looked for all the world like Jackie Kennedy. She was talking about her garden, but the only details I really took in were her own: her shoes, her earrings, her perfect knees.

'So. What do you think?' she said.

'About what?'

'The garden.'

'Fine.' It was the standard lawn surrounded by beds of roses and shrubs. A couple of days to get it into shape and then a weekly mow and weed. She said, 'We don't get the time,' and she shrugged a little sadly. 'I had such great plans for this garden when we moved in, but . . .' and her voice trailed away as if she didn't want to talk or even think about it.

I could come any day I wanted; she worked at home, she said. But I had already assumed that. She seemed so much a part of the house I couldn't imagine her away from it: in traffic jams or in a supermarket or in an office. The house, with its lampshades carefully selected to match the couch which had been chosen to set off the curtains which reflected the carpet, was her domain.

'So when can you start?' she asked.

I was on my way to work with Dick, but before I knew what I was saying I'd told her, 'Right now if you like.'

I didn't want to leave. I had already fallen under her spell.

'Nothing sexier than a bored housewife,' said Neil. I'd wanted to tell someone about Mrs Glover, but I'd made the mistake of telling him.

'It's not like that.'

'It never is.'

'There's something about her. She's got . . . something.' He leered at me.

'For God's sake. She's old enough to be my mother.'

'Ooh, lovely.'

And he was right, she was lovely, and on each occasion I went to her house I found her lovelier still.

One time I was there it started to rain and she told me to come inside to shelter. Again I stepped into the coffee-drugged fug of the house, into the pine kitchen that was so warm and homey it made me yawn. We looked out as the rain drove harder and the windows misted up. 'Oh, let's have some lunch,' she said.

She put soup and hot bread in front of me. 'I'm on a diet,' she said, but then she found some apple pie in the fridge and curled up into a chair like a cat and spooned it lovingly into her mouth.

She peered through the windows at the garden and said again, 'I always wanted to do something with it but . . .' She shook her head. 'It's not my forte.'

'Wouldn't take much to turn it into something,' I said. Why I said that I don't know. I had no plan or anything. But she was interested now. 'Like what?'

'Well . . . we'd need to create some nice curves in the beds; line the walls with trellis; maybe have a pergola going from the terrace down to the lawn; a bird house would be nice; and some fruit trees. You need some shade-loving shrubs on that north-facing bank, and a rockery in the middle would be a good feature.'

I amazed myself at the detail that gushed out of me. Before I'd finished she had pulled out a sheet of paper and was drawing a plan of the new and improved garden. While the rain poured we drew borders and beds, paths and orchards.

A summer house was added, with a hammock on the porch. The lawn, instead of the square that it was now, would curve round beds that we stocked with plants which gave year-round colour. A wisteria spread across one wall of the house, a flaming pyracantha across another. When we'd finished Mrs Glover sat forward with excitement.

'It's wonderful,' she said. 'I want to make this happen. It's the garden I've always wanted.' She had a girl's glee in her voice. I would have found it difficult to deny her anything.

The rain had stopped, and the terrace was steaming. 'I'd better get back to work,' I said. She poured me a coffee to take outside. This time the message on the mug was: Windsurfers do it standing up.

While we were waiting for Dave Allen's response to our latest batch of sketches, Dick and I had decided to write a half-hour script, a sitcom.

'How about something set in a lighthouse?' said Dick.

'How about an ironmongers?' I replied.

'How about an electrical-repair shop that also sells second-hand equipment and parts for vacuum-cleaner models that you can no longer get hold of from the manu-facturers?'

We decided it wasn't about locations.

'It's more about characters,' I said.

'It's also about titles,' said Dick.

'Characters and titles,' we agreed.

'If we can come up with a snappy title . . .'

'And good characters . . .'

'We're halfway there.'

I tried to think of good characters. Dick put his mind to snappy titles. We decided to go downstairs to his pub to do research. It was a cavernous East London saloon, with lots of mirrors and lots of violence. The locals were a friendly bunch who all had jobs that alliterated with their Christian names: there was Dave the Dustman, Pete the Policeman, Phil the Photographer, and Graham the Plasterer who soon saw where he was going wrong and became a greengrocer and never looked back.

When we told them we were writing a sitcom we heard the familiar chorus of: 'Do one in a police station/photography studio/dustcart depot.' But then Harry the HGV driver, who had recently begun a relationship with a woman in Penrith where he drove once a week, suggested we write the story of a long-distance romance. 'Hilarious things happen to people involved in long-distance romances,' he said.

We both liked that. It did seem an original idea. 'We just need a good title,' said Dick.

He phoned me up later that night. '"How about our long-distance-romance couple come from Warsaw?' he said.

'Warsaw?'

'Yeah . . . and they get separated, and the girl stays over there, and the bloke comes and lives over here.'

'Yeah?'

'Then we can call it . . . . *Poles Apart.*'

The man was a genius, and it was a privilege to write with him.

The trouble with – as well as the attraction of – Mrs Glover was she had the kind of charm that made you believe there was no-one who mattered as much as you. An electrician came round one morning to put a light on the patio. When Mrs Glover went inside he whispered to me, 'She's all right, eh.' I almost socked him one. How dare he speak like that about my Mrs Glover? Didn't he know she and I had a special relationship?

But she had charmed the electrician as easily as she had charmed me, and that made me wonder about Dr Glover and how he coped with knowing that every man he introduced his wife to was going to fall for her. Looking around the house, it seemed empty of his presence. There was one picture of him holding a horse for her while she sat on it dressed in full riding gear, but that was the only reference to him I ever saw.

Then in the garage one day I came across a lovingly kept collection of carpentry tools: chisels and saws and planes, all sharp as broken glass, all wrapped in lubricated cloth like surgical instruments. That was the sort of man the doctor was; that was what he did with his spare time. While his wife reclined on cushions and read *Homes and Gardens* of an evening, he came into the garage and made coffee tables.

The electrician said to me, 'You know what I like about her? She's mature. I like mature.'

Later Mrs Glover came out with coffee for the two of us. The electrician's mug read: Golfers don't die, they just lose their balls. Mine: Man about the house.

Neil laughed when I told him. 'She's got the hots for you, it's obvious.'

'No it isn't.'

'If I was selling a financial package to a woman as desirable as Mrs Glover and she gave me a mug that said Man about the house, I wouldn't leave until I had a damn sight more than my 10 per cent.'

'She's a married woman.'

Neil shook his head and smiled in a paternal way. 'It's going to happen,' he said. 'There's no point in fighting it.'

Next time I went round to her she almost grabbed me and pulled me inside. 'There's no point in fighting it,' I said

to myself. But she was excited about something else altogether. She said, 'I've been looking at prices . . . I think
somewhere in the region of £300 should cover it.'

'Cover what?'

'The cost of the garden redesign.'

I stalled. She was serious. 'That's . . . a lot of money,' I
said.

'If something improves the quality of life, it's worth
doing,' and she looked at me in such a way that I realised
there was a good chance she was the most attractive woman
living in Britain at that moment.

I did my weekly session at Lady Brignal's. Helen was upstairs
playing Kraftwerk. I was raking moss off the lawn and saying to myself: if something improves the quality of life,
it's worth doing. If something improves the quality of life, it's
worth doing.

I asked Helen, 'Have you ever had an affair with someone
you've worked for?'

'No. Have you?'

'Not yet.'

She looked worried for me. She said, 'If I was you I
wouldn't even think about it. Work and pleasure don't mix.'

I questioned that theory. Why didn't work and pleasure
mix? It seemed to me they mixed very well. In fact I would
say the more pleasure in a job the harder you worked at it.

'Don't do it,' said Helen. There was a note of fear in her
voice.

'Why not?'

'It'll end in tears.'

There was no answer at the door. I knocked twice but she
didn't come, and yet the car was in the drive. She was in

– she never went out – so I tried the handle and the door opened. I stuck my head in and called hello, still no response. And then through the kitchen window I could see her lying on a recliner on the terrace. I called again. She was asleep.

I walked into the kitchen, dragging my feet in the hope she'd wake, but she didn't move. A paperback lay across her lap, sunglasses had fallen to the ground, sun lotion by her side. Asleep she looked older: her muscles had relaxed, her mouth had fallen slightly open, a sag of skin ringed her neck. But the bottom of her blouse had lifted slightly and the sight of flesh around her waist made my mouth go dry. I watched her for a moment through the sliding kitchen doors, knowing she'd wake as soon as I opened them. I felt like an intruder, a voyeur, I could feel my heart beating and I lost my nerve and turned away. I went outside again and this time banged the kitchen door as I came in, and she sat up with a start.

Her face sprang back into shape. She stretched, thrust her shoulders back and said, 'I feel wonderful after that.'

I didn't see her again for the first hour, but then that familiar smell of fresh coffee escaped from the kitchen, and she came out clutching a mug for me.

She put it down on the low wall near to where I was working, then hesitated. She wanted to say something, but she looked nervous. She jumped as the phone started ringing in the house.

'Phone,' I said.

'Yes.' She seemed unhappy at the idea of speaking to whoever it was. She let it ring a few times, hoping it would go away, but then she turned and strode back across the lawn.

I picked up the coffee, sipped from it, then went back to my weeds. It wasn't until I was halfway through the mug that I saw what was written on the side: 'Coffee, tea or me?'

The garden was suddenly silent. Even the birds were

shocked. I felt tension spread across my shoulders. I glanced round to see if anyone was watching.

What would Neil do now, I wondered. Well, I knew the answer to that. He would have marched in there and gone for closure.

But . . . it might have been a mistake. I had seen her take mugs off the hooks before; she just grabbed the nearest one to her. She'd given me Coffee, tea or me?, but it could as easily have been You don't have to be stupid to work here but it helps.

But she'd never given me Coffee tea or me? before. She'd never looked so edgy either. I glanced up at the house. I could see her, still on the phone, waving her arms about.

Then she put the phone down, and turned and stared out of the window at me, straight at me. I looked away.

All my senses were sharpened. I heard a clock strike eleven somewhere miles away. I heard a bus brake sharply on Haverstock Hill. I felt an ant crawl up onto my arm. I weeded furiously, pulled up anything I could find. I was a gardening machine. Then I heard footsteps on the patio. I froze as she called to me. I took a deep breath and looked up, and couldn't quite believe what I saw: she was dressed ready to go riding.

She had the whole outfit on: jodhpurs, hacking jacket, white shirt, tie, black boots. In one hand she held a helmet and gloves, in the other a riding crop.

All sorts of interpretations flashed through my mind. The last one was that she was about to go riding. 'I'm going riding,' she announced. She sounded irritated. I could only think I had annoyed her by not going in and seducing her.

'If I'm not back by the time you leave, just close the door.'

'Right.'

'Money's on the table.'

'Thanks.'

Then she about-turned and left me, her boots clicking on the stone. I heard the back door close, and the car drive away.

I spent the rest of the session raking the lawn. It didn't need doing particularly, but the very process was cathartic. Some people guffawed when I told them I was a gardener, and they gave a nod and a wink as if I was obviously starring in my own production of *Confessions of a Horticulturist*. And yet nothing of the sort had ever happened to me. As I dragged that rake across the grass, however, I decided this could be one of those experiences I would remember or regret for ever. I needed to act. If she came back I would be forthright. I would be silent and physical. I wouldn't let her down again.

I finished the lawn and spent the next hour ferociously digging over the bottom bed. I dug deep with the kind of energy only lust can generate, as I unearthed soil that hadn't seen the light of day for fifty years.

Then I heard the car pull up.

I plunged the spade into the mud, wiped the sweat off my brow, washed my hands in the pond and headed for the house.

There in the kitchen stood Dr Glover. 'Where's my wife?'

'I don't know . . . She's gone riding.'

'Riding!' He seemed astonished. 'Riding?'

'That's what she said.'

'She hasn't been riding for years!' Now he was suspicious of me. 'What are you doing in here anyway?'

'I was just finishing; I came to get my money.' He looked at me unkindly. His bedside manner had deserted him. 'I really wish you hadn't shown her that garden design,' he said. 'She's got it into her head now. It's going to cost me thousands.' He dug his hands deep in his pockets. 'It's become an issue.'

Suddenly everything had an explanation: her nervousness; the phone call; her anger; her jodhpurs. I didn't belong here any more. I took my money and got out.

Over the next fortnight I had a few more cups of coffee from Mrs Glover, but nothing suggestive ever again. One mug didn't have a slogan on it at all, it was just plain blue. She was being distant. I felt jilted.

She never spoke about the new garden design again, either. She always seemed to be working when I went round. Then one evening Dr Glover phoned me at home and said he didn't want me to come any more. He didn't offer an explanation and I didn't ask for one, in case he said, 'For lusting after my wife, you bastard!' or something similar.

Being sacked convinced Neil that I had actually succeeded in seducing Mrs Glover. He tried to comfort me, bless him. 'So you lost the job, it's not the end of the world. I've lost loads of deals that way. Bet it was worth it though, eh?'

'I never touched her!'

'Oh, come on.'

He was never going to believe me. I found it hard to believe myself. But I discovered a way to get over the disappointment of it all.

Dick and I had begun work on our radical new sitcom *Poles Apart*. In the first episode the young Polish man comes to England. He becomes a gardener and he falls for the older woman who employs him. They resist each other until one day she grabs him in the garden shed . . .

And the way we wrote it, Neil was right: it was worth getting the sack for.

13

GINGER AND YOUNG 'UN

Mr Gold called at his usual hour and informed me he had just bought a new property and the garden needed attention. It hadn't been touched for a year or more; it would need the best part of a week's work.

'I can manage that,' I said. I liked to keep Mr Gold happy. Not only was he a good employer, he once showed me how to repack the bearings in the wheel of my bike.

'There's one snag,' he added. 'The house is in Norfolk.'

He had been passing in his car, and seen the For Sale sign. It was all so idyllic he couldn't resist it. He'd bought it to add to his rentable range, but so taken was he, with the village and the house, he thought he might just keep it as a holiday home for his family. His suggestion was I went up there for a week to do the work, stay in the house. 'The place is yours,' he said.

The way he spoke it sounded like the holiday I'd thought I would never get that summer. 'I'll go next week,' I told him.

He was very pleased. He said, 'All I need now is a decorator. Any ideas?'

I had a wonderful idea: I'd ask Helen to come with me. I put it to her straight. 'How about a week decorating a thatched cottage in Norfolk?'

'Who with?'

'A lovely idyllic village.'

'Who with?'

'By the sea . . .'

'You mean with you, don't you?'

'A purely professional arrangement, of course. Listen, a free holiday I'm talking about here . . . yes, with me.'

So it was Pete the painter and me, driving out to Norfolk one sunny August morning, Pete's van loaded up with paint and the lawnmower Gold had given us. I'd taken him round to meet Gold. Pete had turned on the charm. 'Oh I love Norfolk,' he said. 'The mustard, the turkeys; my godmother comes from Norwich.'

He'd been disappointed when Mr Gold handed him a dozen tins of Buttermilk paint.

'There's a very interesting blistered aubergine on the market at the moment, Mr Gold. Nice silk finish.'

'Buttermilk's fine.'

'Mango yellow? It's very subtle.'

'Buttermilk.'

Pete still hadn't given up hope of educating the general public in their choice of interior decor, but he certainly wasn't going to let it get in the way of a free holiday. He loved the idea of a week out of London as much as I did. 'I've always fancied moving out of town,' he said dreamily. 'Norfolk is the place to paint. Big-sky country. Think of all the great artists who came from Norfolk . . .'

'Like?'

'. . . I can't think.'

When he picked me up he was wearing a flat cap and a corduroy jacket. He had wellingtons in the back. 'You've got to fit in in the country,' he said. 'People will talk about you if you don't.'

We drove north up the A1. 'I always wanted a job with travel,' said Pete, as we whizzed round the Peterborough ring road.

After lunch he pulled into a lay-by and insisted we listen to *The Archers*.

'Why?'

'That's all they talk about in the country. We've got to be informed. It's no good going into a pub and talking about *Coronation Street*.'

After it was over Pete turned the radio off and said, 'Did you understand that?'

'Not a word.'

'Nor me. I think this week is going to be more of a challenge than we imagined.'

We pressed on through Wisbech and King's Lynn. The land began to flatten. We fell silent as we crossed the fens and a sense of alienation grew. I'd been in London all summer and I felt uneasy surrounded by all this countryside. The harvest was ripe, the land parched, and the sky full of seagulls.

The coast appeared like a mirage in the distance, a gentle slope of land that merged almost imperceptibly with the sea haze. And then we were driving down narrow lanes into the village, a flint and brick-coloured jumble of cottages, with a church, a pub and a Post Office shop, and not a single person on the street.

In the window of the Post Office, among the faded tins

of carrots and boxes of fudge, was a sign that read: Half Day Closing Today.

'Ah, that explains it,' said Pete.

'Explains what?'

'Where everyone is.'

'Where?'

'I don't know where, but if it wasn't half-day closing the whole place would be . . . brimming.'

We looked around. You couldn't imagine this village brimming.

'They'd be in here buying their tinned carrots and jigsaws and fudge like you wouldn't believe,' said Pete. 'I mean, if it was open I'd buy a jigsaw.'

We found Mr Gold's property, a flint cottage with peeling window frames and five-foot-high thistles in the front garden. A honeysuckle had wrapped itself round the door in such a knot we had to prune our way into the house.

Inside it was dark and musty. The water and lights worked, but there was no furniture. Each footstep echoed.

'Just what I expected,' said Pete, determined to enjoy himself. 'Open the windows, dry the place out, be fine. We're in the country now.'

Upstairs were two little bedrooms. 'Bagsy the master suite,' said Pete.

'Which one's that?'

'The one without the dead jackdaw in the fire grate.'

I opened my bedroom window and looked down onto the back garden. The summer had encouraged it to run riot. The grass was knee-high. Foxgloves towered above a tangle of weeds. The hawthorn hedges reached for the sky. Behind the beds was a vegetable patch that had gone to seed, and some fruit cages with nets torn and doors swinging. Gold had said he had furniture arriving next week, and was coming for a holiday himself with his daughter and children the week after that. There was a lot of work to be done before then.

Pete strolled around saying things like, 'He should knock this wall down and have a ranch-style kitchen, then take out the staircase and . . .'

We rolled out our sleeping bags, put our toothbrushes in the bathroom, spread our stuff about in an attempt to make the place feel less empty. Then with nightfall the house came alive with creaks and gasps. I looked at Pete. Pete looked at me. At that moment the lights went out. One of us might have screamed. 'Let's go to the pub,' said Pete.

Instead of saying hello, the landlord greeted us with, 'No food on a Monday.'

We ate peanuts and pickled eggs and drank beer that came from London. Pete tried to be friendly. 'This pub reminds me a bit of the Bull at Ambridge,' he said.

'Where's that?' said the landlord.

'You know,' said Pete. 'The Bull . . . at Ambridge.'

'Never heard of it,' said the landlord, and went back to reading the previous day's paper.

Pete tried again. 'So. How old is this pub?'

'I don't know,' said the landlord, then screwed up his face and asked, 'Are you birdwatchers?'

'No,' I said.

'Good. Bloody birdwatchers.'

We told him we were working on a house in the village and he grew less suspicious. When we told him which house, he actually became interested. He said, 'Ginger and Young 'un used to live there.'

Ginger and Young 'un were twins who moved into the village forty years ago. Neither of them had married. They looked after themselves, worked for the council, and then on retirement put their heart and soul into the garden. For years they dominated the local horticultural show with spectacular flowers and vegetables that no-one could equal. They were eighty-six years old when Ginger had a fall, went into hospital and died. Without him, Young 'un – the younger brother by forty minutes – slipped into decline. He was put into residential care a few months later and died of pneumonia just before Christmas. They were buried next to each other in the churchyard.

'Holiday home, is it?' asked the landlord.

We told him it was going to be.

'Be full of bloody birdwatchers.'

Back at the house we spoke in whispers. 'Place is haunted,' said Pete.

'Don't be ridiculous.'

'Haunted by twins. It's the stuff of nightmares.'

We looked out of the window at the moon shining on the lawn. It didn't take much imagination to make out the figure of a ginger-haired man digging in his vegetable patch, his younger brother by forty minutes tending to the gooseberries.

The moon lit up the garden shed with a silver glow. I said, 'Did you know the best time to plant parsley is in a full moon at midnight?'

'Bollocks,' said Pete.

It was hard to sleep. Pete was right, the ghosts of the twins were all over the house. At some small hour I heard noises on the stairs and waited for twinned apparitions to float through the door. I lay on the floor wrapped tightly in my sleeping bag and wondered which twin slept in which room. Who did the cooking, who did the cleaning? One grew the vegetables, the other the flowers. I imagined them waking on their birthday and Ginger giving Young 'un a pair of gardening gloves, Young 'un giving Ginger a grass rake. I eventually fell asleep thinking how hard it would be to gift-wrap a grass rake.

Next morning, the dawn burst through the curtainless windows and Pete burst through my bedroom door. He said, 'I had an amazing dream. About Mr Gold. He gave a sign.'

'What sort of sign?'

'He was telling me how he didn't really want his walls painted Buttermilk. He wanted a scene from Norfolk life, a rural mural splashed across the living-room wall.'

'A rural mural?'

'A rural mural.'

'I like the sound of that.'

'So do I.'

'No no. I like the sound of "a rural mural", but I don't like the sound of a rural mural.'

Pete looked at me, confused. 'Did you hear the ghosts last night?'

'Yes.'

'So did I.'

We managed to stop a milkman and get some bread and milk and eggs, and Pete cooked up while I went to explore the garden.

It may have been neglected, but beneath the rampant brambles and grass the beds were well stocked. Flowers were trying to force their way through, plums were falling off a tree in the middle of the lawn, and in the wrecked fruit cages birds gorged on berries. Mr Gold had told me that the garden shed and all its contents had been left with the house, largely because no-one could find a key to the padlock. I had to unscrew the latch to get in. The rusted door fell open, sending a gang of spiders rushing for cover. Inside was a mesh of cobwebs with a thousand flies hanging out to dry. An array of ancient tools leaned against the wall in retirement. On the work table was a half-full pot of compost, and an open packet of seeds. It was as if someone had left in a hurry. Ginger had fallen while watering the tomatoes, Young 'un had heard his cry, heard the watering can hit the ground, and rushed to help.

And then I saw a snapshot pinned to the wall, a curled, sun-bleached photo of two men – undoubtedly twins – taken in the garden. They were standing before a backdrop of bloom – the beds at this time of year – and one of them, Ginger by the look of him, held three pale red gladioli in his hand, just cut. He held them up – prizewinners no doubt. The picture caught a moment full of life and hope and pride. And now it was all gone, faded away. It was the most emotional moment I had ever had in East Anglia.

A sudden urge to restore the garden overcame me. It was all there after all, it just needed to be set free. So I went on the attack with my pruning saw, became ruthless – cruel to be kind. I started a bonfire and fed it all day. A plume of smoke rose straight up into the still sky.

Slowly I began to notice wildlife: a woodpecker hammered away in the woods; a heron loped across the next-door field; a squirrel scampered into the garden and scampered out again. It was as if I had woken something up.

Quickly the features of the plot reappeared: a curve of a bed here, a wigwam of beanpoles there. And then islands of colour surfaced, waving: a bed of roses, a clump of dahlias. And there were the gladioli, sheltering behind the green-house, not smothered at all, but standing straight and proud, chins reaching for the sun. Some had been attacked by pests, but they were blooming nonetheless. They were red, pink and white, and pure white, and all squealing, 'Pick me, pick me.'

I collected a bag of plums and took them in to Pete. The local radio was blaring away. 'Guess what?' he said. 'Three cases of salmonella in Great Yarmouth this week.'

His dream had got the better of him. From somewhere he had found a pot of slate grey and was drawing a wind-mill on the living-room wall.

'What are you doing?'

'I told you; Mr Gold asked me to do it.'

'No he didn't.'

'Yes he did.'

'Phone him up and check.'

'No . . .'

'He'll go nuts.'

'I can't stop now!'

The letter box rattled and a flyer floated through the door. It was the brochure for the village horticultural show, to be held that weekend. Entries from all comers were invited for all categories. Everything from a jar of marmalade to three carrots (heads on). And there, halfway down the page for cut flowers, was Category 68: three cut gladioli.

That evening, on the way to the pub, we took a stroll round the graveyard. The grass had just been mown and the pollen made me sneeze and sneeze again. A woman tending to a grave looked up and said, 'Bless you.'

We hunted round the tombstones, looking for the twins' graves. Pete said, 'Whenever I come into a graveyard I remember I want to be cremated.'

'Why?'

'You're just surrounded by dead people in a graveyard. It's depressing.'

'Where are you going to have your ashes scattered?'

Pete looked stumped. 'I hadn't thought. That's a good question.'

We didn't know the twins' surname so we asked the woman if she knew Ginger and Young 'un.

'Of course I do,' she said, and led us down to a corner of the churchyard. And there they were, together as always. One simple headstone, the names Ginger and Young 'un – the only ones they seemed to be known by – carved on the stone.

'Are you relatives?' she asked.

'No, we're just . . .'

She looked at me. Just what? Ghouls?

'We're just staying in their house,' said Pete, deciding honesty was best. 'I'm painting it and he's gardening it.'

'They were wonderful gardeners,' said the woman. 'The village show isn't the same without them.' Then she rolled her eyes and said, 'I suppose Morris Topham will win all the prizes.'

'Who's Morris Topham?'

'Don't ask.'

We went to the pub and ordered sausage and chips and peas. Pete said to the landlord, 'So I hear Morris Topham is going to sweep the board at the horticultural show.'

The landlord sneered. Morris Topham wasn't much better than a birdwatcher in his book. 'Morris Topham needs to have some respect,' was all he'd say.

'This is more like it,' said Pete. 'We've stumbled across gossip and rumour and local contention.'

The sausage and chips came. The barmaid said, 'Do you want a knife and fork with that?'

We stayed until closing time. Three people came in. One to drink a pint of lager and take two hours over it; one to ask directions; and another to pick up the man drinking the pint of lager. We found ourselves speaking in whispers. The loudest noise in the place was the strange click that came from the landlord's hip as he patrolled the bar. 'Quiet tonight,' I said to him when I went to get another drink.

'We used to have background music,' he muttered. 'But the parish council banned it.'

On the way home Pete said, 'Under an oak tree in a meadow by a cool river.'

'What?'

'That's where I want my ashes scattered.'

That night the ghostly noises came again. Pete crept into my room. 'Can you hear that?' His voice was shaking.

'It's just the pipes.'

'Well the pipes are coming up the bloody stairs, if it is.'

I got up and went out onto the landing. There were no ghostly twins there, just a marmalade cat. 'It's ginger,' I said to Pete, and he whimpered and ducked under my sleeping bag. 'He's come back as a cat.'

Pete painted the rest of the house Buttermilk as requested, in the hope that he would get away with his rural mural in the living room, which now covered one wall and half the ceiling. He was very pleased with it. 'I keep telling you. Norfolk is the land of big sky.'

I spent all my time tending to Ginger and Young 'un's gladioli. I said to Pete, 'I think it says something about the nature of gardens, that they keep on flowering when their gardeners are dead and gone. Like dogs waiting at the grave-side of their dead masters, these gladioli are pining for the nurturing hands of Ginger and Young 'un.'

'This gardening lark's gone to your head,' said Pete.

The gladioli had gone to my head. They were coming into

their prime. The previous week had been wet, now the sunshine fuelled them. They were reaching their zenith as they always did, right on schedule, in time for the show. I began to feel a great sense of responsibility. Just who did Morris Topham think he was?

We had been in the village four days now and Pete's idyllic view of the countryside was beginning to pall.

'Still haven't met any women.'

'So?'

'I thought there'd be country girls all over the place.'

He decided to buy the parish magazine. 'There might be a social page.'

There was, but the only event was a WI talk. Having Fun with Fish, by Betty Dennison. All welcome.

'I'm up for that,' said Pete.

'It's not what you think it is.'

But we couldn't sit in the pub another night. And Pete was convinced Fish was a euphemism for an altogether more illicit evening, one they couldn't possibly publicise for fear of attracting the local constabulary, something that would end up with local women dancing on tables.

We turned up in the village hall at seven thirty. We were the only men. Pete wore his corduroy trousers and jacket in which he thought he was irresistible, but no-one spoke to us. We sat in the front row and Betty Dennison got up and welcomed everyone and nodded in our direction, then spoke for an hour on all the wonderful things you could do with fish, which were kind of interesting but weren't exactly 'fun' as billed. The audience was very respectful, only two falling asleep. The applause at the end lasted fourteen seconds according to the village-hall clock.

Afterwards tea and biscuits were served. Pete stood in

the middle of the gathering smiling at everyone. He said to me, 'Do you get the feeling they're waiting for us to go before they bring out the drugs?'

Eventually a woman with a goldfish-shaped badge in her lapel approached us. We explained what we were doing in the village. 'Oh, Ginger and Young 'un's house,' she said. 'What will the horticultural show do without them?'

'Where does Morris Topham live?' I asked.

She curled her lip at the mention of the man's name, and backed away from us.

That night the house banged and sawed as if Ginger and Young 'un were putting up shelves downstairs. I lay in my bag and read the parish magazine by torchlight. Enid Willis had just gone into hospital; the village football team had lost 13–1 in their opening match of the season; a ladder with two rungs missing was for sale. And there, in the bottom corner of the back page, was an advert: Open Garden, all this week. The Pink House. Morris Topham.

The Pink House should have been easy to find, but it wasn't, because it was blue. Although, in fact, it was any colour you wanted it to be, so overflowing was it with flowers. Hanging baskets hung, climbing roses climbed. Creepers crept over the garden walls. The beds were brilliant with dahlias and chrysanthemums, and the lavender borders were so rich the whole garden smelt like the cosmetic department in Debenhams.

Tending to his beds was Morris Topham. He had a face as red as a fuchsia and he gardened in a shirt and tie. Pete said hello. Morris Topham said, 'Have you put 10p in the box?' He indicated a collection tin. 'Proceeds to the Horticultural Society annual outing.'

We each put in 10p and went to inspect his vegetable

patch. It was laid out in neat troughs with labels and sticks. There was string marking out the rows. String featured a great deal in Morris Topham's garden, defining lines beyond which no flower dared cross. There was something joyless about the whole thing. Morris had turned his garden into a production line. When I found his gladioli they summed up the philosophy underpinning this little garden city. They were perfect and upright and each leaf was sharp and firm. They looked like beauty queens, right down to their smugness and fixed smile. They looked as though they had popped pills, as though they were surgically enhanced. If they could answer a question they would say something stupid. I wondered, if Morris Topham keeled over in his garden today and died, whether his gladioli would pine for him the way Ginger and Young 'un's did for them.

When we got back home I watered my gladioli, pulled out a single weed that had rooted between them. I knew there was only one thing to do. I had to enter them against Morris Topham's in the horticultural show the next day.

Pete supported my plan. He had decided to enter the show as well, in the 'original piece of rural artwork' category. As I cooked up some spaghetti on the camping stove that evening, he sat out in the garden and searched for inspiration. Then he started drawing. He worked for three hours and produced a picture of a handsome cow. On one half of the beast he had depicted a carton of milk, on the other, a half-pound of Country Life butter. The picture was called *Buttermilk*.

'You don't think that's a little avant garde for this village?' I said.

'On the contrary, it will awaken the post-modern spirit that I am convinced lies simmering beneath this community.'

Ginger and Young 'un ran round the house and banged

pots and pans with excitement all that night. 'Shut up for God's sake!' shouted Pete. It made no difference. They knew show day was dawning. I finally got to sleep at first light, when rain started to fall and the soft patter on the tiles sent me off.

In the morning the birdbath had filled and the garden looked refreshed. I was worried the gladioli might have been damaged by the rain, but they were in a sheltered position and looked as happy as ever. I sneaked up on them and cut three down — one of each colour — with a quick snip, a simple amputation. It was their destiny.

In the village hall entries had to be out on the tables by ten o'clock. Home-made cakes were being handled like fine porcelain. Two entrants almost came to blows over damson jam. Pete and I filled out entrants' forms. Category 68: three cut gladioli. Name of Entrant: Ginger and Young 'un.

Everywhere in the hall was evidence of Morris Topham. His mud-free crop was displayed like items in a supermarket, all scrubbed roots and cellophane. They looked as if they had make-up on. He had entered just about every category except number 81: most strangely shaped vegetable — none of Maurice Topham's vegetables were anything but straight. He had brought his own lights, and now he was arranging them to show off the best side of his onions.

Pete put his drawing on display. He was very confident. 'There's only two other entrants,' he said. 'I'll clean up.' The prize money for first place was 20p.

The village was indeed brimming that Saturday. Folk had dressed up. The pub was busy, the landlord said, 'Bloody customers.' We sat in the pub garden and watched the judges file into the village hall. They were an independent jury, bussed in from another village. They were all above board.

The judging started at eleven o'clock, and results were

to be ready at twelve. Morris Topham came and sat in the pub to wait. He looked nervous. He didn't drink. His wife sat next to him sipping ginger wine and leaving mauve smears of lipstick on the glass. A clock struck midday and I overheard someone say, 'It doesn't get much more exciting than this.'

We hurried back over to the village hall. There was a queue to get in and a 20p entrance fee. 'Proceeds to the Horticultural Society annual outing,' said the man on the door.

The trophies were lined up on a table at the far end, and all around the room rosettes and certificates had been placed by the winning entries in each category. There was a crush to get to the front. I caught a glimpse of the leeks, huge cartoon-like specimens: first prize Morris Topham. Then the carrots: first prize Morris Topham. Roses: first prize Morris Topham. It was the same wherever I looked: potatoes, beets, dahlias, sweet peas. Without competition from Ginger and Young 'un, Morris Topham's pristine produce had triumphed.

The biggest crush, though, was round the gladioli. I pushed my way through to see. 'Who would have thought it?' said a stunned onlooker.

'It's the first time that's happened,' said another.

'I'm not sure if it's allowed,' said a third.

They were referring to the fact that Ginger and Young 'un had won first prize in Category 68: three cut gladioli.

'Dead people can't enter!' complained Morris Topham loudly, not taking defeat gracefully.

He appealed to the committee. The committee conferred and announced there was nothing about it in the rule book. Ginger and Young 'un were the official winners. I went up to collect the prize. I said, 'Ginger and Young 'un couldn't be here today due to another engagement.' No-one laughed.

I was given a certificate and a little brown envelope

containing my 30p prize money, which I immediately donated to the Horticultural Society annual outing. 'Where are you going this year?' I asked the secretary. 'The Raj Indian restaurant in Cromer,' he informed me.

Morris Topham gathered up his clutch of trophies in a trolley and wheeled them out. Then the raffle was drawn for a luxury hamper, and his wife won it. Only Pete seemed upset with the day. First prize in the rural-drawing category went to a watercolour of the Great Yarmouth roller coaster. Second prize went to a drawing of Morris Topham. Despite only three entries the judges had decided that Pete's effort wasn't worth third place.

Pete looked hurt, quite understandably. 'I've a feeling I don't fit in here,' he said.

The day was quickly over. Anything left behind was auctioned off. I bid for some beetroot, I don't know why. They were my souvenir of the week.

I took the gladioli away and on the way home we called into the graveyard again, and I put the flowers on Ginger and Young 'un's grave in a milk bottle of water.

Mr Gold visited the next day. Pete showed him round the house, saving for last the living room, where his rural mural had grown into an epic landscape covering three walls and all the ceiling, and involving windmills, castles and a distant seashore. Gold said, 'It's very good. I like it. Better get rid of it now.'

'But . . .' said Pete.

'Buttermilk,' said Gold.

He was happier with the garden. I told him he needed to get someone in on a regular basis to maintain it, and he said he'd already found someone. As long as it wasn't Topham.

We had our last night in the pub. After the excitement of the previous day it had reverted to its familiar inert state. There was no food and no customers. 'Everyone's exhausted,' said the landlord. 'Takes us a week to recover from the horticultural show.'

That night the ghosts of Ginger and Young 'un left us alone. All was silent in the house. The first prize for their gladioli had set them to rest.

We went back to London the next day, travelling with a sense of anticlimax. Pete had been quiet most of the way, but as we joined the queue of traffic heading back into town along the A12 he said, 'I've changed my mind. I think it's got to be off Tower Bridge.'

'What has?'

'My ashes scattered. I'm a city person. Know what I mean?'

14

HERMAN GAPP

Back in London everyone seemed to be on holiday. Mandy from downstairs went to the Algarve for a week with five suitcases. Helen had gone on a short tour of Wales with a open-air production of *A Midsummer Night's Dream* in which all the cast wore anoraks. Neil went to the Lake District, to stay in a monastery. He sent me a card: *satisfaction-of-self arising from the resourceful attainment of one's set aim in the cognisance of a clear conscience. Wish you were here, Neil.*

It was the end of August. Hampstead Heath was littered with foreign students rolling about in the long grass. The fair arrived for the bank holiday weekend. The only people still working were myself and Powerflowers.

All summer I'd seen the sharp edges of their white van disappearing round corners as they cruised the Holly Lodge Estate like a team of predators, hunting for gardens to neutralise. I saw a copy of their catalogue once. It featured pictures of the styles of gardens customers could choose from: Mexican Ranch, Italianate, or Chinese Willow.

Although it didn't matter much which one was picked, the result was always a monument to cement and bark chip.

Since the mystery of my stolen bicycle wheels our relationship had consisted of making faces at each other, but then they overtook me one afternoon as I struggled up Highgate Hill. I heard one of them shout, 'Want a drink?' and an empty carton of juice was lobbed at me.

I yelled abuse back at them, and went home and wrote a sketch where a bullied David-like figure gets the better of his own personal Goliath with the aid of a sharp wit and a lot of explosives.

'Powerflowers have touched a nerve, haven't they?' said Dick.

They had, and if he'd told me the day would soon come when I desperately needed their help, I wouldn't have believed him.

There were many impressive houses around the edges of the Heath: towering, Gothic piles that lined the avenues up the hill to Hampstead Pond, and newly built villas that lay down cul-de-sacs – architects' dream houses made of glass and steel with solar power and kitchens on the top floor.

The most attractive location of them all was Millfield Lane. There, behind high walls and electric gates, were mansions with gravel drives and views looking down over the swimming ponds and the wide expanses of the Heath on into the West End.

I was always amazed when I was asked to call at houses like these. Passing through gates where money didn't seem to be a concern, I had to fight the notion I was stepping back into the upstairs-downstairs era. I imagined these places would have teams of gardeners who lived in, were provided with overalls and died aged seventy-five digging over the potato patch.

Mrs Gapp lived in such a house. She answered the door wearing a pale blue jellaba which hid her feet and made her look as though she was rolling around on wheels. She seemed so pained when she spoke of her previous gardener, Ronald, I thought she was going to swoon. 'He was such a treasure,' she sighed. 'He was with us fifteen years,' and she shook her head in disbelief. I assumed Ronald had died in some dreadful gardening accident, or maybe he'd decided to end it all with a bottle of weedkiller. But no, he'd gone to live in Tewkesbury. 'I don't know what we'll do without him,' she said, making it clear Ronald was going to be a hard act to follow.

The house was modern and looked as though it had been built to order. It was mostly made of glass. The front wall of the ground floor was one big sliding window that gave access to the garden, and on the first floor was the living area and a veranda where you could sit and watch the sun set over the distant city.

The garden went all around the house. It had a diamond-shaped lawn, a shrubbery, and a small orchard. Mrs Gapp led me to a bed of hydrangeas in full flower. 'Hydrangeas were Ronald's favourites,' she said with a sigh, and stuck her nose into a pink bloom. Then she took me to the shed and said, 'Ronald used to like to sit in here and have his lunch.'

But Ronald had a cushy little number, if you asked me. The garden was wonderfully low maintenance. The lawn was in good nick and there was a top-of-the-range mower to cut it. The shrubs were all well contained. The only flowers were roses; and all the beds had ground cover – hypericum and periwinkle – which kept the weeds down.

The only tricky zone was the orchard, but when I questioned Mrs Gapp she said, 'We have a specialist come once a year to take care of the fruit trees.' It was no wonder Ronald found time to sit in the shed.

I arranged to go once a week for a morning. I'd mow the lawn, and deadhead the roses, then hide behind the compost for a bit, until at eleven o'clock Mrs Gapp would call, 'It's ready.' And I'd go in and sit in her well-fitted kitchen and have coffee and two biscuits.

The house was open-plan and looked a bit like a gallery, with many large pieces of art: sculptures on plinths, abstract paintings – blue bleeding into yellow into pink. There was a lot of leather. I sat dunking my shortbread, wondering where their money came from.

There was also a large collection of books. Bookshelves stretched along two sides of the living room, and one needed a stepladder to get to the top. I would have loved to have spent a morning browsing through them, but after five minutes Mrs Gapp would come back to the kitchen and say, 'It's getting brighter,' which after a couple of visits I realised was code for 'Get out of here and back to work.'

Then one morning as I was putting my wellingtons back on I said something extremely banal, like, 'What a lot of books!' And she said something equally banal designed to get me out of the house, like, 'Yes.'

'Where do they all come from?'

'Herman's clients mostly,' she said.

I wasn't sure what this meant. I stood on the doorstep looking quizzical. She knew the quickest way to get me back to work was to tell me what her husband Herman did.

'He's an agent,' she said.

I looked blank: travel agent, estate agent. Then it dawned on me she meant writer's agent.

'Oh,' I said, and grinned. Dick and I would have prostituted ourselves for an agent.

'What sort of writers?'

'All sorts. The hedge needs trimming today.'

'Like TV writers . . . ?'

'Yes of course.'

I spent the rest of the morning gardening on autopilot, thinking: if her husband is this wealthy on the back of his writers, just imagine how wealthy the writers themselves are.

Afterwards I pedalled straight round to Dick's pub. I told him I was gardening for a literary agent. He said, 'Did you say you were a writer?'

'No.'

'Thank God for that!'

'Why?'

'People like him can pull the plug on our career before it's started.'

'He's an agent!'

'Listen to me. You have got to understand that Herman Gapp, and all his sort, don't want people like you and me breaking into writing. We don't want to go near them. Once again you have been seduced by your day-job environment. I worry about you.'

'We need an agent!'

'We do. But not one like that. We need an agent from . . . the streets.'

'We need an agent who will sell our script. We should show it to him.'

'Over my dead body!'

This attitude was unhelpful. It was also paranoid. I decided to show Herman Gapp our script anyway.

*   *   *

I made a photocopy of *Poles Apart*. Then I took it to a printer to put a fancy binder on it. 'What is it, anyway?' he asked.

'It's a sitcom,' I told him, proudly.

'About what?'

'A young man from Poland who's seduced by an older woman.'

He wasn't impressed. He said, 'You should write a sitcom about a printers, mate. It's hilarious some of the things that happen here.'

My plan was simply to give it to Mrs Gapp and ask her if she could possibly show it to her husband, because we would really value his professional opinion. But when I knocked on the door Herman answered it himself.

He said, 'The gardener, right?'

'That's right.'

'Good. I want to talk to you.'

He was a wiry man with a lot of freckles, and he leaned forward too far when he walked so he had to move quickly to stop himself falling over.

He led me round to the back of the house and scrambled up the bank behind the shed to the only patch of the garden which wasn't cultivated. It was a steep incline and covered in brambles. He said, 'This is a mess. I don't want mess. You know what I want?'

'What?'

'I want it terraced. You understand? I want it turned into three or four different levels. And I want logs driven in along the edge of each level to keep the earth in place. And then I want little gravel pathways in between the levels. And I want plants planted: heathers and stuff.'

'Good idea.'

'It's all yours.'

'You want me to do it?'

183

'Course I want you to do it. You're a bloody gardener aren't you?'

I didn't want to appear incompetent or unindustrious. I wanted to appear keen and full of imagination so that he'd think to himself, 'This guy is so sure of his ability he'd probably be able to turn his hand to anything, scriptwriting even.' So I said, 'Sure. No trouble.'

'I'll order the gravel.'

'Great.'

'And wooden stakes.'

'Fine.'

'You'll just have to do the digging and banging.'

'Suits me.'

He was at home because he and his wife were packing up to go on holiday for two weeks. 'You reckon you can do it in the time we're away?' He looked me straight in the eye. I hesitated. I had the script in my hand, 'Two weeks should be fine.'

'Good,' and he shook my hand as if the deal was done, and just as he was about to turn away I shoved the script at him. 'I wonder . . . if you'd like to read this.'

'What?'

'This. It's a script.'

He looked at it as if he didn't know what I was talking about. 'Where did you get this?'

'I wrote it. With a friend.'

'You're a writer?'

'Yes.'

'What sort of script?'

'Sitcom.'

'Good thinking. Sitcoms are where the money is.'

'I wondered if you'd like to read it.'

He looked at me as if I was a pile of dog dirt. Then he

took the script, weighed it in his hand and nodded. 'It feels funny.'

I laughed.

'Not that funny.'

'It's our first.'

'I'll read it on the beach.'

'Great.'

He moved closer to me, gave me a snarl disguised as a grin and said, 'I'll let you know what I think . . . when I get back from holiday.'

And I knew then that Dick's and my future as writers now depended on what sort of job I did on Herman Gapp's terracing.

I started as soon as they left for Spain. They gave me the code to the electronic gate to let myself in so I had access to the garden whenever I liked.

I'd been to the library and read up about terracing and discovered it wasn't as straightforward as it looked. The experts recommended you cut as many levels as possible. And it was no good just digging up the top and barrowing it down to the bottom, you needed to make sure you redistributed the valuable topsoil evenly, so it spread over the whole bank. And you never sank the border stakes in a straight line: you gave them a curve to avoid uniformity of design. Obviously.

This was all good advice, but after one morning it was clear the job was going to take twice the time that I had. If I was to get it finished within two weeks I would need to work nights. I put the rest of my gardening on hold, told people I was ill. I stopped going round to Dick's to work. I shovelled earth until it got dark each night; even so it didn't seem to make much difference. After a week I was standing in a pile of mud and rocks, looking at the picture in the library book of the perfectly terraced garden, and wondering whether the Gapps would be able to trace me if I did a runner.

Eventually I finished one level and carted a whole bunch of split logs up to hold it in place. I piled them up on the pathway, then dug a trench to stand them up in. It was tough work, but by evening I'd dug deep enough. I stood back to admire my effort, and that was when I knocked against the logs and sent them all rolling down the hill, gathering pace, until they ploughed straight into Ronald's shed, smashing in one side of it and giving the entire structure a tilt to the west.

I looked at the wreckage and saw my career slipping away with the sunset. I needed help.

Dick didn't flinch when I explained the situation: that I had gone behind his back and given *Poles Apart* to Herman Gapp to read on holiday and in return I had wrecked his garden. He just nodded soberly, stroked his formidable chin and said, 'You've screwed up.'

'I have.'

'There's only one thing for it.'

'What?'

'I'll have to help you.'

I looked at him, carefully. Did he mean he was going to help me in the garden? Yes he did. 'Oh, there's no need for that,' I said.

Dick isn't the sort of person you want working in your garden. His problem is he's happy with everything the way it already is. A bed full of weeds looks fine to him. A lawn can have grass knee-high or be shaved so it bleeds and he's indifferent. Brambles? Fine. Greenfly? Great — wildlife!

Smashed-up shed? Looks rustic. He has a blasé relationship with everything he knows nothing about, and near the top of that list is gardening. To him, a window box is the thing that new windows come in.

But I was desperate. I had asked Neil and he'd said, 'I don't get out of bed for less than £5 an hour. And I want insurance and holiday pay.'

There was no-one else. So Dick turned up the following morning.

His only previous visit to Highgate was the time he had fallen asleep on a night bus. He seemed uncomfortable in such surroundings. 'People with burglar alarms are terminally stupid.'

'Why?'

'Alarms are like signs outside the house saying, "We've got lots of valuable things in here." If I was a burglar I'd only burgle houses with alarms.'

He kept asking me names of plants and when I didn't know he looked appalled, not at me, but at the idiocy of the people who employed me. 'If someone comes into my pub and says, "What drink's in that pump?" I have to know. I can't say, "I'm not sure; it might be beer, it might be gin; or it might be something I don't know the name of."'

'It's written on the bottle or the tap, isn't it?'

'The name of these plants is written on a label round their necks.'

'They're in Latin.'

'Well how stupid is that?'

He shook his head a lot that morning. He seemed baffled with the whole idea of the activity. But he was fascinated with the range of gardening implements the Gapps owned. I told him to clear out the shed so we could try and repair it, and he kept picking up tools and saying, 'What's this?'

'It's a hoe.'

'What do you do with it?'

'You weed with it.'

He looked at it for a while, turned it round, examined it closely. 'I don't get it,' he said.

'It's a bloody hoe!'

'You already told me that. How does it work?'

'You hoe with it.' And I grabbed it off him and gave him a demonstration of hoeing.

'Who's this?' he said, finding a photo of a man I assumed to be Ronald.

'It's the previous gardener.'

'Where's your picture then?'

The work wasn't progressing any faster. Clearing out the shed took all morning. For all his concern about our script, Dick didn't seem that worried about getting the job finished. At lunchtime he said, 'Right, where's the cafe?'

'This is Highgate; there are no cafes.'

'Course there are cafes.'

He led me off in search of a cafe for lunch. And much to my surprise we found one, in the parade of shops at the bottom of Swains Lane. We had egg beans and chips and tea, and sat among bus drivers who came in from the terminus across the road for their breaks.

Dick read the racing forecast in the paper. I looked out of the window and saw the white van of Powerflowers pull up outside. I thought they were coming in, but they crossed the road and lurched into the pub opposite.

'So they're Powerflowers?' said Dick, intrigued. He weighed the situation up, and then as we left he marched over to the pub.

'Where are you going?'

'Business.'

He wasn't there long. He came back across the road to me and said, 'I've been speaking to your bitter rivals. I pretended I needed some terracing done and a garden shed repaired. They said £50.'

'£50!'

'Cash. No questions.'

'That's outrageous.'

'That's what I told them. They said take it or leave it.'

There was no decision. I wasn't paying anyone twice what I was going to earn for the same job. I started walking back up the hill.

'Hang on,' said Dick. And then I realised he was eyeing the bookies.

'No,' I said.

'I've got a winner. Charlie's Angel in the two o'clock at Epsom.' He looked at his watch: one fifty-five.

Five minutes later we were in the neon-lit, litter-strewn den of the betting shop, listening to the two o'clock at Epsom, with £5 of my money on Charlie's Angel at 13–2.

Five minutes after that we were walking back up the hill again. 'Can't understand it,' said Dick. 'He should have romped home.'

We worked through the afternoon, barrowing earth, knocking in logs, flattening off the paths. But the shape of the terrace wouldn't come. It was a mess. It was all mud and bits of string. Gapp was due back the day after next and his terrace looked more like a building site than a garden feature.

Dick was exhausted at the end of the day as I led him into the Flask at the top of Highgate Hill. We had a pint while the young brokers sauntered in after a hard day in the City making a fortune on the stock market.

'We are in the wrong business,' I said.

'Don't be fooled by that lot,' said Dick. 'They won't look so smug when Herman Gapp has sold three series of *Poles Apart* to the States.'

Then he downed his pint, wiped his mouth on his sleeve, and climbed on a 236 to Hackney Marshes.

Helen's open-air production of *A Midsummer Night's Dream* in anoraks returned to London to play one night in Stoke Newington. I didn't tell her I was coming along. I just turned up and sat on the grass.

The idea of the entire cast wearing different-coloured anoraks was an interesting and particularly British one, supported by the audience who had entered into the spirit of the occasion and dressed in a range of outfits from Barbour jackets to dustbin liners. Helen played a yellow-hooded Titania, who was enamoured by the 'amiable cheeks' of a Bottom despite the fact that he was hidden inside a bright red kagoul. All this was tempting fate, of course. With the amount of waterproof material around, rain could pour with impunity. And that was just what it did. '"I love not to see wretchedness o'ercharged,"' said the Queen of the Amazons, bringing the play to a close, and she stood there dripping while the audience ran home.

I met Helen afterwards. 'It was a disaster,' she said.

'No it wasn't; it was good.'

'You're just saying that.'

'I'm not.'

'If you did think it was a disaster would you tell me the truth?'

'No . . .'

'What would you tell me?'

'I'd tell you it was good.'

'See.'

'It was good!'

I was surprised her boyfriend hadn't come to see the play.

'Michael doesn't like Shakespeare. He thinks he's over-rated.'

'Bit harsh.'

'He thinks Shakespeare never really tackled the issues.'

'Hmm . . .'

'Michael takes himself very seriously.'

This sounded like a challenge. 'I take myself seriously as well.'

'I'm sick of men taking themselves seriously.'

We waited at a bus stop. 'Actually,' I said, 'I don't take myself all that seriously.'

She suddenly did an odd little jump, and made a noise that sounded like a small animal being run over.

'What was that?'

'A sneeze.'

'Never.'

'Don't.'

'That was the strangest sneeze action I've ever seen.'

'I'm very self-conscious about my sneeze.'

I couldn't help laughing, and she took a swipe at me. 'I'm not laughing at your sneeze.'

'What are you laughing at then?'

'I'm laughing at the little details I'm slowly getting to know about you.'

'What details?'

'Your sneeze . . .'

'And what else?'

'Nothing else. You've got to start somewhere.'

A man in an anorak joined us. He saw Helen and said, 'Didn't I just see you in the play?'

'Yes,' she mumbled, in the manner of Greta Garbo.

And we both waited for him to say how wonderful it had been, or how he'd thought it was a disaster, or how the trouble with Shakespeare was that he didn't tackle the issues, but he said nothing like that. He said, 'Is that your own anorak?'

'Yes,' said Helen.

'I've got one like that at home. Except it's blue. It leaked a bit round the seams so I rewaxed it. Good as new now.'

We took a bus to Holloway. I gazed into the window, at Helen's reflection. She looked back at me and said, 'You're looking serious now.'

I was feeling serious, thinking about Herman Gapp and his terrace. 'My future is balanced on a knife-edge,' I told her. 'This time tomorrow I might be a very rich man. Or I might be on the run.'

It was an enigmatic thing to say, but it suited the scene: two people alone on the top deck of a steamed-up bus with rivulets of rain running down the windows. She shivered and moved closer to me. Just as I was thinking about kissing her, she jumped and sneezed again. 'I think I'm going down with something,' she said.

The next day Dick was late, and when he did turn up he was a bag of aches and moans. He sat down in the chair in Ronald's shed and sucked a mint.

'Are you all right?'

'I reckon Herman Gapp might just like our script so much he won't bother about the garden.'

He was looking for an excuse for an early lunch.

'He's due back in twenty-four hours,' I said, and handed him a shovel.

I pushed him hard during that morning. We drove in more stakes and started to lay the gravel. I pulled out the remaining brambles from the edges by the wall. But then it started to rain. Hard. Within minutes the place was flooded and mud was floating down the new paths, taking the gravel with it. We sat in Ronald's shed and Dick read the book I had from the library. 'Make sure you lay pipes at the bottom of each terrace for drainage.' He looked at me. 'Have you laid pipes for drainage?'

'No.'

'Why not?'

'Couldn't be bothered.'

'You're a bloody cowboy.'

'I know.'

'This is going to be a disaster! He's going to sue you.'

'If he can find me.'

'I think the situation calls for more drastic action.'

He marched me back down to the betting shop. And demanded another £5 off me. I was too depressed to resist. He put it on a horse called Do It Yourself in the twelve thirty at Catterick.

'Trust me on this one,' he said.

I didn't care any more. I'd give up gardening, I'd take up window cleaning instead.

Do It Yourself came in at 12–1.

'Stroke of luck,' said Dick.

He collected our winnings and marched across the road to the pub.

'Where are you going?'

'Business,' he said and then I saw the Powerflowers van parked outside.

'I'm having nothing to do with this.'

They came round straight away. For £50 cash they happily abandoned whatever job they were working on. I couldn't bear to be there. I went onto the Heath and sat on a bench by the boat pond, and watched an angry man try and ram ducks with his remote-controlled battleship.

It didn't take them long. I saw them leave just before six o'clock. I peeked round the corner of the gates to see Dick sitting in Ronald's shed reading the paper.

Behind him the slope had been sliced into neat terraces. Gravel paths lined the spaces between. The wooden supports had been knocked into place, creating a pleasing curve. They'd even put plastic pipes at the bottom of each terrace for drainage.

The panels in the shed had been seamlessly repaired.

'They were a nice bunch of blokes,' said Dick. 'They farted rather too much, but they were a laugh.'

'They don't have the personal touch, though.'

'Bollocks to the personal touch.'

'Look, they've dropped cigarette ends.'

'Well, that can be your job, collecting the cigarette ends.'

'They can't possibly have done it in that time. There must be something wrong with it.'

'Listen, mate. Tomorrow, when Herman Gapp buys our script for a huge sum, and I get a trophy wife and a big house in Chigwell with a whacking great garden, I'm going to employ Powerflowers long before I employ you.'

Before we left, Dick took one last look round the grounds and said, 'Although, when I move to Chigwell I reckon I'll do the gardening myself. It's a piece of cake.'

Next morning as I cycled to work I passed kids in uniform waiting at bus stops. A little chill went through me as I realised schools were back, and another summer was over. And when I looked more closely the signs were everywhere. Leaves were already turning on the big chestnuts on the Heath. The ice-cream seller had gone. Mrs Lavenham had stored her garden furniture the day after the bank holiday.

I did two hours for her that morning, preparing her beds for autumn pinks. She said, 'This is fun, isn't it?'

She was beaming, but it wasn't just the joy of working with fresh manure. Something else had made her day. 'Oh, by the way,' she said trying to be nonchalant. 'Have I told you? Edward has sold his book.' And she glowed with pride.

'His book on Pope Pius?'

'No. No, he decided on a change of tack. He's written a Western. It's very good. It's called *Death at Deadman's Gulch*, I think.'

If Edward could sell a book we could sell a script, I reckoned, as I freewheeled down West Hill and turned off to the Gapps. Their car was in the drive. The curtains were drawn back. They were safely home.

I flattened my hair, brushed my knees and knocked on the door. Herman tugged it open as if he'd been waiting.

'Ah!' he exclaimed, then paused, clearly having forgotten my name. 'The gardener. Wonderful.'

'How was Spain?'

'Great. Good. Well, it was all right. Rained. I got food poisoning. Virginia got stung by a jellyfish. Do you know what the best part was?'

He was going to say our script. He was.

'Coming home and seeing our new terrace. Well done. Damn fine job. You even put drainage in, I see.'

'That's right.'

'Looks just how I wanted it . . . leave it now the summer's over, put some plants in in the spring . . . that purple stuff that tumbles down and some of those little white jobs.'

'Good idea.'

He smiled at me. I smiled back. He said, 'I know what you're looking at me like that for . . . you want paying.'

And he took out his wallet which was bulging with cash, and whipped out thirty quid. 'Here. Bit extra for a job well done.'

'Thank you . . .'

'Well . . .'

'I just wondered if you managed to read our script?'

'Ah. Yes. Your script. Yes. I read it.'

'What did you think?'

'I think . . . you should stick to what you're good at.'

'What's that?'

He laughed: 'Gardening, of course!'

AUTUMN

15

JASPER

Bernie at the garden centre was worried about the nights closing in. 'It means less time spent in the garden,' he said. 'It means less money spent on garden furniture. It means a drop in demand for barbecue equipment. It means I'm never going to get rid of these damned ice creams.'

He wanted my help to plan for the coming autumn months. He imagined that I had my finger on the pulse of the average gardener, that I knew before anyone else what gardeners wanted and when they wanted it. 'You spend all day with them,' he said. 'You have an intimacy with your customers that a shopkeeper dreams of. You can be my marketing guru.'

I would happily have helped, but any needs I identified in my clients were rarely of a gardening nature. I knew Annie Kendal needed a weekend away from her kids. I knew Nugent needed a tall blonde. And as for Mrs Fleming, it was clear she needed medication.

'You know that Robin Day?' she said to me.

'On the radio?'

'He brings me out in a rash.'

'Mrs Fleming!'

'They should push him off a bridge.'

She'd been having more and more of these unreasonable rants, on a range of issues.

'And what about McVitie's?'

'McVitie's?'

'The biscuit people!'

'What about them?'

'There's something very odd going on down there.'

There was something even more odd going on inside her head. I turned up one morning and she said, 'What are you doing here on a Sunday?'

'It's Tuesday.'

'Oh.'

Once I found her watching the horse-racing on TV and she told me she was related to Lester Piggott and never missed him if he was on the telly. When a different jockey won the race she said, 'I'm related to him as well.' Another time she told me to make myself a cup of tea and I opened the fridge to get some milk and found it full of shoes.

Then came the day she answered the door wearing headphones. She had become the proud and enthusiastic owner of a metal detector. 'I ordered it from the catalogue,' she shouted. '£23.50 with batteries.'

She had quickly become convinced there was buried treasure in her garden. My job was to trail round after her with a trowel. Whenever she got a signal in her headphones she would stop and shout, 'There!' and I would have to dig deep until I unearthed the precious metal beneath, which invariably turned out to be a nail or a tin-can lid or a milk-bottle top.

Occasionally I would dig up a ten-pence piece and this

encouraged her hugely. 'It's just a matter of time,' she would say.

'What is, Mrs Fleming?' I asked once. 'What exactly are you looking for?' But by then she had her headphones back on and was oblivious.

The metal detector fed her delusions of grandeur and she became obsessed with it. She produced a book on local history and came to the conclusion her house was built on the remains of a Roman camp. 'There must be all sorts of coins and jewellery right under our feet.'

The garden became littered with piles of earth. All the rusty 'treasure' we found was stored in the downstairs bath and then washed off and examined, but afterwards instead of being dumped it was put on shelves and displayed. Mrs Fleming's inability to throw anything away was clear from the first time I walked in the house, but lately things had got out of hand. Once she asked me to take a box upstairs for her and put it in the bedroom. But I couldn't find the bedroom. There was nothing, like a bed, to distinguish it from any other room. The room she called her bedroom was crammed with lampshades and buckets.

It was hard not to smile, but it was also worrying. There was no-one to look after her, no family or friends. The telephone never rang. She never left the house as far as I could see. She had been my first ever client, and over the six months I'd been gardening for her I'd seen her grow steadily more confused. I asked her if the neighbours ever called, but she didn't seem to know what I was talking about. On one side were flats, on the other was a house with the curtains drawn. If they did know her they had probably decided long ago that she was someone to avoid.

Then one morning I arrived to find the front door open and all the windows thrown wide.

'Giving the place a good air,' she said. 'Bit of a clean.' The very idea was astonishing — dust held her house together. To clean it properly would have involved the emergency services. I opened the back door to find the lawn covered in rugs, pots, stuffed animals, pictures — the detritus of thirty years was spread all over the grass. Her plan was to empty the house.

She wanted me to do the same with the garden shed, but it quickly became clear that my task that morning was to get everything back inside before the rain came. I shook the rugs and curtains that she'd draped over bushes. I dragged chairs and tables back indoors. One box contained nothing but odd bits of broken china. 'Shall I throw them away?' I asked her.

'I'm going to mend them all at the weekend,' she said.

We just managed to beat the rain. She seemed satisfied. 'I should do that every ten years,' she said. Then I went round the house helping her close the windows and we sat and had tea as the weather set in for the day.

She asked me, 'Have you seen Jasper?'

Jasper the tortoise? No, I hadn't seen him.

'He's not eaten his lettuce.'

Outside, a bowl of lettuce was left untouched and was slowly filling with water. 'That's very strange,' said Mrs Fleming, putting on her wellies.

I followed her outside. The rain had left the first smell of autumn in the air. 'Jasper!' called Mrs Fleming, and she started to hit the shrubs with a stick, as if she expected him to come bounding out of the bushes like a puppy. Then she spotted the back gate onto the lane was open.

'Who opened that gate?' she shrieked and, as usual when there was any trouble, she pinned the blame on me. 'You know that gate is always kept closed.'

She had most likely opened it to air the garden when she opened every other door, but she quickly jumped to the conclusion that she had had intruders.

'You can't be sure,' I said. 'There's nothing missing.' And if there was she'd never be able to say what.

'Of course something is missing,' she snapped. 'Jasper.'

Her wild eyes grew even wilder. I could see this quickly getting out of hand. I closed the back gate firmly and said, 'Let's just check the garden, shall we?'

We started at one end and moved systematically down to the back wall, looking under every stone, parting the vegetation, peering under shrubs, under pots stacked against the shed. It was odd, because Jasper was normally the easiest of animals to find. You just looked under your feet and there he was about to be crushed, but this morning there was no sign of him.

Mrs Fleming screamed, 'They've stolen him! I know it!'

'Why would anyone want to steal Jasper?' I said.

'There's a black market in tortoises,' she said. 'Don't you know anything?'

Maybe he had escaped. I went out into the lane and looked up and down the road for a runaway tortoise. Jasper didn't seem like an adventurous sort of creature — tortoises rarely do — I couldn't imagine him running away any more than I could Mrs Fleming going to see *The Cars That Ate Paris* at the Hampstead Everyman. But there across the road was the Heath. Maybe he'd plodded out of the garden he had known all his life and heard the call of the wild. If so, he could be halfway up Parliament Hill by now. The alternative, of course, was he'd become a meat pie under the expensive wheels of one of Mrs Fleming's neighbours.

'I'll have to call the police,' said Mrs Fleming.

I managed to distract her from doing this by pointing out

a hole at the bottom of the garden wall. It had been burrowed, and was smooth and deep enough to accommodate a tortoise.

Mrs Fleming said, 'He wouldn't go next door.'

'Why not?'

'He doesn't know them.'

'He's a tortoise!'

'They've also got a wild dog.'

I marched Mrs Fleming round to her neighbours. The door was opened by an elderly gentleman with a Yorkshire terrier under his arm. Mrs Fleming took a step back. I explained we were on a mission to find a tortoise.

'A what?' said the neighbour, with a French accent.

'A tortoise!' I repeated.

He shook his head. 'A what?' and he fiddled with a hearing aid.

'A tortoise,' I said, more loudly. 'With a shell.'

He smiled a smile that said: one of us is crazy and it might be me.

I mouthed the words very slowly, 'A tortoise,' and did a very poor mime.

'A tortoise?' he said.

'Yes, a tortoise.'

'Ah. A tortoise,' he nodded knowingly. 'How much?'

When I managed to convince him we weren't selling one but looking for one, he introduced himself as Mr Rimes and happily let us search his garden. Mrs Fleming, who had never met Mr Rimes before, walked round in shock. Four inches of brick was all that separated her jungle from this showpiece of paving stone and wrought-iron furniture. The open space must have made her feel agoraphobic. There was certainly nothing to attract a tortoise in here – there was little shade and little to eat. If Jasper had wanted to lounge on an ornate chair or swim with some carp in pond water that looked clean enough to drink, he'd have been all right, but if he was after habitat, this garden was a desert.

Mr Rimes sneezed and his Yorkie yapped. He said to Mrs Fleming, 'How long have you lived next door?'

'Thirty-two years,' said Mrs Fleming. 'How long have you lived next door?'

'Only nineteen,' said Mr Rimes.

'Well I'm pleased to meet you,' said Mrs Fleming.

'I've been meaning to introduce myself,' said Mr Rimes, and when he saw us out he shook Mrs Fleming's hand and said, 'I hope we can do this again.'

I tried to get Mrs Fleming to cultivate the friendship. 'You could be company for each other,' I suggested.

But Mrs Fleming gave a shiver and said, 'He was foreign.'

'So?'

'He'd want to go on outings to the Zoo and places.'

She called the police in the end. They arrived just before I left. Mrs Fleming led them to the scene of the crime and explained her loss.

'A tortoise?' said the officer.

'Not just any old tortoise,' said Mrs Fleming. 'He was a Turkish Eggshell. Worth a lot of money on the black market.'

'You told us you had a break-in.'

'You don't understand. He's been stolen.'

The officers stood on the terrace with their hands in their pockets, both thinking: mad as a barrel of monkeys. They glanced round the outside of the house, at the rotten window and door frames, and announced it was probably the least secure property in the whole of North London. Then they told her they'd keep their eyes open, but not to get her hopes up, and they left shaking their heads.

'Makes you want to take justice into your own hands,' said Mrs Fleming, rather alarmingly.

When I told Neil he said, 'She should have had better insurance.'

'You can't insure against losing your tortoise.'

'Course you can. Home Contents.'

'Jasper lives outside.'

'Garden furniture comes under contents.'

'Just because a tortoise moves slowly doesn't mean it's furniture.'

'I bet you I'm insured against tortoise theft.'

'You haven't got a tortoise.'

'You're right. However, I may have friends visiting for the weekend who bring a tortoise with them. Besides, I might get one. They're a good investment, I understand.'

What was all this about the value of tortoises? And where was this market where shady characters asked you if you wanted to buy one, no questions asked?

Hampstead Heath was quieter now. No kites flew above the hill. The swimming ponds began to turn green and unwelcoming. The smell of bonfires drifted across from Kenwood House. You could look up at a leaf and will it to tumble. I saw Glenda Jackson in an overcoat.

I also saw a tree with a poster on it. 'Lost – probably stolen – one Tortoise. Name of Jasper. Tortoise shell colour. Last seen September 18. Reward for information leading to his return.'

Posters had been stapled at regular intervals along a trail that led to a lamppost on Mrs Fleming's road, then to her front window where a shrine to the missing Jasper had been assembled: a candle and a photo in which he looked like every other tortoise you'd ever seen.

Inside, the house was like mission control. Mrs Fleming sat at a desk with a map. She had had three phone calls so far, she said. All of them wondering what the reward was. They had hung up when she'd told them it was her collection of *National Geographic* dating back to 1967.

But she wasn't demoralised. In fact she seemed reinvigorated. I couldn't believe that she'd gone round the Heath herself and put the notices up. 'I did it one night,' she said proudly. 'I walked across the Heath with a torch. No-one mugged me.' A mugger would have run a mile if he'd seen Mrs Fleming's silhouette heading his way. She was beginning to look like William Hartnell as Doctor Who.

My job that morning was to roam the Heath looking for Jasper. 'I'll stay here and man the phones,' she said.

To search the Heath was a ridiculous thing to do, but if it made her feel better then why not. I hunted in the undergrowth within a hundred yards of the house, thinking: Jasper, mate, why did you run away? You had it made.

A dog was barking at me. It was a Yorkshire terrier on one of those retractable leads. Far away on the other end was Mr Rimes. He waved as he shuffled over to me. He was dressed in a camel coat and scarf, and his dog had a little camel blanket wrapped round it that made it look like a sausage roll.

'How's Mrs Fleming?' he asked.

'She's all right,' I told him. 'Actually I don't know if she is all right. She needs someone to check on her now and again.'

'I can do that,' he offered. 'I've got a ladder.'

'You could just knock on the door.'

'Good idea. As long as it's not on a Wednesday evening. That's Neighbourhood Watch night.'

A week passed. The posters began to blow across the

Heath, the ink running in the rain. I went to the garden centre and said to Bernie, 'I've got an idea for you. You should sell tortoises.'

'Why?'

'Because . . . a client of mine has lost hers and I reckon if I buy her a new one she won't know the difference.'

Bernie wasn't convinced. He was looking for the kind of item he could stack high and sell cheap. He was about to buy a job lot of plastic garden gnomes; he thought they'd be perfect Christmas presents. He wanted to use them in a window display.

'Give a gnome a home,' I suggested.

'That's brilliant!' said Bernie.

Mrs Fleming began to look very tired. I wondered if she was eating. Mr Rimes went round and visited her, and asked if she wanted anything from the shops. She'd told him she wanted a forty-watt bulb and a mousetrap.

'He means food,' I told her. 'He'll go to the shops for you.'

'Oh I've got plenty of food,' she said to me, and she showed me her larder. It was stuffed with hundreds of tins of beans with sausages, and fruit salad. She could have survived a nuclear winter.

Another week passed; still no sign of Jasper. Mrs Fleming read a book on the Galápagos and discovered turtles there lived for hundreds of years. She started to laugh and said, 'That's where he's gone, where tortoises live for ever.'

I asked Mr Rimes if he was still looking in on her and he said, 'I called yesterday afternoon. She stuck her tongue out at me.'

'She's got an odd sense of humour,' I told him. 'Don't abandon her.'

But the next time I called Mr Rimes saw me pass by his front window, and he came hurrying out. He looked frightened. 'She's gone,' he said. 'They took her away yesterday.'

'Took her where?'

'In an ambulance. There's a woman in there now.'

The woman was a social worker. She was collecting some things for Mrs Fleming. I told her I was the gardener. 'I suppose I'm a friend as well.'

Mrs Fleming had been found on Hampstead Heath one night with her metal detector. The police were called, and when they asked where she lived she'd told them the Galápagos.

They had taken her to the police station, where she was assessed by a mental-health team and taken into hospital.

'I'm looking for her handbag,' said the social worker.

I shrugged. 'Could be anywhere.'

I helped her look for a while, moving boxes, newspapers, books. 'No next of kin?' I asked.

'She has a sister,' said the social worker.

I was amazed to hear this. I had assumed Jasper was her nearest relative.

'She lives in Kentish Town.'

That was just two miles away.

The social worker lifted up a box, jumped and gave a little shriek.

'What is it?'

'It's a tortoise.'

Jasper must have climbed in a box that day when Mrs Fleming emptied her house onto the lawn. I was in such a hurry to get everything back inside I hadn't noticed him in there. He'd been trapped for two weeks. He'd survived on lumps of cardboard. He looked weak and slow, but that was how tortoises always looked, and he quickly perked up once he was back in the garden. But who would look after him now?

Mr Rimes was happy to have another pet. 'I will watch out for him,' he said, dutifully. 'I shall make sure he is still here when Mrs Fleming comes home.'

He widened the passage under the wall so Jasper had better access to both gardens. By the entrance he put a nice plate of mixed pre-washed salad from Marks & Spencer, and a water bowl that looked part of a thirty-six-piece willow-pattern dinner service.

'I hope Mrs Fleming gets better soon,' he said. 'I am going to ask her to a Neighbourhood Watch meeting. Or maybe for a drink in the Freemason's Arms.'

'She'd like that,' I said, and I had this wonderful image of him walking down the road with Mrs Fleming on his arm. She'd have her bow legs and patched jacket; he'd have his walking stick and camel coat; and they'd be heading off to the pub for a gin and tonic and then on for a meal at Claudio's Trattoria.

Although, if I was honest, I didn't expect Mrs Fleming ever to come home again.

16

MRS CHESTER

'It's October,' said Dick.

'So?'

'So if we haven't sold anything by Christmas we're giving up . . . remember?'

I didn't want to think about it. Back in the spring the deadline we set ourselves had seemed so far in the future I imagined we'd have sold whole shows' worth of scripts by then. I felt a poke of panic. 'I've got an idea for a sketch about an outsize-shoe shop,' I said.

'How about an outsize-shoe shop staffed entirely by escaped convicts?'

And off we went again. We wrote and we wrote. We sent off parcels of stuff to Dave Allen. We heard the Two Ronnies were doing another series so we wrote pages of one-liners for them. Then a show called *Not the Nine O'Clock News* wanted material. It featured the new wave of comedians who had made names for themselves on the fringe, doing for comedy what punk had done a few years earlier for rock music. Like the punk rockers they crossed over into the mainstream before long, but we loved *Not the Nine O'Clock News*, and we sent them our favourite stuff: a man goes into a bank and asks to withdraw some money, but the cashier says, 'Sorry sir, we had a robbery last night and they stole your money.'

'What? Just mine?'

'Yes. They took your box.'

'What box?'

'The shoebox we keep your money in, under the big bed out the back.'

Actually, money wasn't a problem. If I got short I just readvertised in newsagents' windows and extra gardening work would come in. I was in control, and I still imagined it was just a matter of time before we wrote the perfect joke and money poured in. Riches by any other means seemed unlikely, but this was before Mrs Chester in Muswell Hill had a funny turn, and then suddenly it was gardening rather than writing that offered the chance of wealth.

I'd been gardening for Mrs Chester throughout the summer, and the single word to describe her was *mean*. Everything about her, from her screwed-up face to her chicory-flavoured coffee, advertised the fact. She rolled her eyes when reports of famine came in on the news. Her bird table had mouldy bread on it — 'I'm not giving bacon rind to them!' She said spiteful things about her neighbours. I'd always have to ask her to pay me and when she did it was in loose change, money she'd dug out from behind the sofa. She was bigoted, insensitive, reactionary, a pessimist, a bully and a misanthrope.

She was also very rich.

Her house was like an antique showroom, a collection of paintings, silverware and porcelain, all lovingly dusted and

polished. Most of the rooms were dark because of all the mahogany, but they sparkled in corners from the displays of precious metal. The house was hushed and cushioned. The only noise was the enormously valuable grandfather clock ticking laboriously on the landing.

Mrs Chester also had money invested in the stock market, something she took great pleasure in telling me about. She would sit on the terrace wrapped in a darned cardigan reading the newspaper, and call out how well her shares were doing. She shook her head in disgust at the national news pages, but she chuckled her way through the business section.

Her favourite pastime of all, though, was arranging how she was going to dispense her wealth when she died. She had three children, and the most fun she could have was to bring down her big box marked Important Documents and spend the afternoon tinkering with who was going to get what. When I asked what the meaning was of the yellow label marked Fiona, on the fine sideboard that she kept in her garage wrapped in blankets (there was no more room in the house), she told me everything she owned had a label on it bearing the name of its intended recipient. The labels were colour-coded: yellow for Fiona, blue for Philip, red for Robert. 'Saves arguments later,' she said.

The sense of power this gave her kept her going, because the labels weren't permanent – they could be changed. The oak bureau had been earmarked for Robert, but, if he was remiss in his duties in any way, he could easily lose out. 'The useless boy hasn't phoned me for two weeks!' Mrs Chester would complain. 'He'll regret it!' She said it with a laugh, but she wasn't joking. Robert's red label could easily be peeled off the bureau and stuck onto a saucepan, and Philip's blue take its place.

Then one morning I called and a young woman opened

the door to me. She had to be Mrs Chester's daughter Fiona
– the same suspicious eyes, the pinched lips. She explained
that her mother was ill, and she was taking care of her. I
should work as usual.

The curtains upstairs were drawn. The house was quiet
and still, with a solemnity that gave it a chill. During the
morning a doctor arrived, then a man I presumed to be one
of her sons. The family were gathering. I imagined them
around the bed, their mother explaining her colour-coded
system of inheritance one last time.

Mid-morning the son brought me out a drink. I guessed
he was my age, but he had the shoulders and jowl of an
older man. He stood on the lawn in his suit and surveyed
the garden as if he was an estate agent.

'Is your mother all right?' I asked.

He twisted his lips. 'She's not very well . . . but she's a
tough old bird.' There was little affection in his voice. Being
a tough old bird didn't sound like something to be admired;
it was just going to make her live longer. It was the thing
standing between him and the Japanese prints with his name
on. Mrs Chester was so tight she wasn't even going to die
without a struggle.

The driveway was full of cars when I left. 'Shall I come
next week?' I said to Fiona, and she had a think about it
before telling me to leave it for a fortnight, then call in and
see. 'Give your mother my best wishes,' I said.

'I will.'

'One more thing.'

'Yes?'

'You haven't paid me.'

It was around this time I discovered Highgate Cemetery. I
used to go in and find a bench and have my sandwiches.

Along the main paths the graves were mostly cared for, some with fresh flowers and the grass clipped. But, away from these, the plots had become a tangle of brambles and fallen branches. Headstones had crashed into each other and ivy was strangling them. Families visited for a while, but then probably died themselves and the graves were forgotten. If ever a patch of ground looked like it needed a gardener this was it, but, of course, this neglect was the cause of its beauty and charm. It reminded me of some ancient city, abandoned and left to nature. You could get lost in here, the only sound the birdsong and the crackle of sticks underfoot.

Leaves were beginning to fall. The paths were sodden and slippery. The woods smelt of damp. The deep reds and browns added to the sombre atmosphere. Through the trees I could see a burial under way. It was almost two weeks since I had last been to Mrs Chester's, and I managed to convince myself I had chanced upon her funeral. I edged closer. I could recognise none of the mourners at this distance, just hear a mumble of prayer from the priest. The gathering stayed ten minutes and then dispersed. The gravediggers moved in. I closed my eyes in respect for a moment and I imagined Mrs Chester already complaining about her new neighbours.

The next day I made a point of going round to her house, half-expecting to have to offer my condolences to her family. But it was Mrs Chester who opened the door to me! She looked frail and she'd lost weight, but she had a defiant sparkle in one eye, and a raised lip that said: I'm not dead yet, buster!

'It's you,' she said.

'How are you?'

She seemed surprised I should ask, and suspicious of me showing concern.

'I've not been well,' she announced. 'I could have a relapse any time.' She seemed excited at the prospect. 'I thought you were my daughter . . . although I should be so lucky.'

'I was worried about you,' I said, and again she looked confused, trying to discover my motive for saying such a thing. She panicked and said, 'The lawn needs a last cut,' and she left me alone.

I worked hard. I mowed the lawn in perfect stripes. I deadheaded the roses and cut back any perennials that had finished. The least she could have was a tidy garden to gaze upon. I caught her looking at me once or twice during the morning, something she'd never done before, and then she came tottering out to me with a coffee. I hurried towards her to help and was surprised to see that, instead of the usual handful of broken biscuits from the bottom of the tin, the plate she was carrying held two Jaffa cakes.

She handed them to me clumsily. 'I shouldn't be walking,' she said. But then she passed her eye over the garden, something else she'd never really done before. She seemed to be taking an interest.

'What are you doing?' she asked.

'Just making it tidy, for the autumn. Most things have stopped growing.'

She nodded. 'Do you have parents?'

'Yes.'

'How often do you see them?'

'Every . . . so often.'

'My children ignore me.'

'I thought they were here all last week?'

'When they saw I was at death's door. They were all round here to get their hands on . . .' And she stopped herself. I looked away.

'But where are they now?' she went on. 'That Philip disap-

216

peared back to Birmingham as soon as I sat up in bed. And Fiona said she'd come round every day. But where is she?'

I didn't know what to say. She sighed and turned and almost stumbled, and I took her elbow and helped her back inside to a chair.

'I wonder, would you pass me down my box?' she asked. I reached up to a shelf and brought down the Important Documents box. It was heavier than I imagined it would be and hit the table with a crash.

She looked at me as if to say: you can go now.

The trouble was, much as I tried to fight it, I couldn't help but feel sorry for this cantankerous, selfish, malevolent old bag, and as I left that day I thought I should offer her some help. I found her in the kitchen, still working on her documents, writing away feverishly. 'I was wondering if there was anything I could do for you?' I said.

She immediately closed the box, on her guard again. 'Like what?'

'Anything. Any errands. I'm going past the shops on Swains Lane if you want anything.'

And then I saw her do something I never thought I'd see. She blushed; she was embarrassed. And I'm not sure if a little moisture didn't appear in her eye.

'Well . . . I do need a prescription,' she said.

After that I found myself calling more frequently. I did shopping for her. I went to the post office. I took her library books back. She offered to pay me, but I refused to take anything. I said, 'You deserve to be looked after.' She smiled coyly. She gave me another Jaffa cake.

I told myself I was doing it all out of kindness, out of care for a little old lady. But I was only fooling myself. Mrs Chester's disaffection with her children had provoked a

217

meddling with her Important Documents box on an unprece-
dented level. She spent entire afternoons crossing things out
with bold strokes of her fountain pen. She laughed and she
raged, and I knew she was writing them out of her will.
Slowly, the notion began to grow that if I played my cards
right, I could make some money here.

It wasn't such a fantastic idea. Stories about gardeners
being left millions in wills were often featuring in newspapers. With her family out of the way, who else would she
leave it to? Certainly not a friend. She was the sort of woman
for whom life was a game of one-upmanship, and the last
thing she wanted to see was someone she knew profit from
her death. Nor was she the sort who gave to charity.
Christian Aid envelopes dropped through her door and went
straight into the bin. She didn't have a cat to leave her money
to, either, or a parrot. I reckoned I was next in line.

I found myself behaving in a solicitous manner. 'What a
nice blouse, Mrs Chester. Is it new?' I wanted to be the
child she wished she'd had instead of that thoughtless brood
she called her own. I tutted when she told me about their
behaviour. 'Their father's anniversary, and not one of them
phoned me. The man who brought them up. The man who
bought Robert his first made-to-measure suit. Are they
grateful? Not a bit of it.'

I sighed, implying that I called my own parents twice a
week and took them out to the theatre every other weekend;
sent them cards on their birthdays, wedding anniversary,
Mother's and Father's Day, even Valentine's Day.

I took some mending to the dry cleaners for her. I bought
her her *Daily Express*. As I became more familiar with the
house I began to covet items. I imagined her writing my
name on green labels and sticking them under pieces of
furniture. I saw the family gathered in the solicitor's office

after the funeral, the will being read, their astonished faces as the announcement came: 'I've decided to leave it all to the gardener!'

One day I said I'd cook her lunch. She sent me down to the stores for a tin of tuna fish and some frozen peas. I cooked her a tuna and pasta bake and then sat down with her to eat. She looked so frail, as if she could pop off any moment. 'I don't know what I'd do without you,' she said. 'You and Tina, of course.'

'Tina? Who's Tina?'

'Tina's my cleaner. She's an absolute treasure.'

This was disastrous news: I had a rival. And cleaners had far better access to their clients. Cleaners were left money in wills even more often than gardeners.

'What day does Tina come?' I asked.

'Every Friday. She's cleaned for me for fifteen years.'

Fifteen years! Tina had a long-service record as well; the odds of being named chief beneficiary were greatly in her favour. But I wasn't giving up. She wasn't going to get all the loot. I was going to give Tina a contest. I'd split it two ways if needs be. I decided I had two options: 1) I could do away with Tina. 2) I could step up my offensive. I opted for 2, combined with a subtle smear campaign.

Next time I called, Mrs Chester complained her eyes got tired if she read, so I offered to read to her. She handed me a library book called *The Wandering Clouds*. On the cover was a picture of a raven-haired woman in the arms of a Clark Gable-type man. A thunderous sky spelt trouble behind them.

I put some effort into it, gave the characters voices, anything to impress upon her that I cared.

I found my attention wandering round the room, eyeing up the porcelain figurines on the mantelpiece. They were the kind of things I had an urge to take a baseball bat to, but I knew a few places down the Portobello Road which would give me a good price.

'What nice porcelain, Mrs C.,' I said.

'Royal Doulton.'

'Of course.'

'Do you collect porcelain?'

'I am but a poor gardener.'

'Don't worry,' she whispered. 'Your ship will come in.'

After two chapters she said, 'I think I've read this book before: she leaves him and marries the chauffeur.'

I laughed and picked up another book: *The Wind Calls his Name*. On the front cover was a picture of a blonde-haired woman in the arms of a Burt Reynolds-type man. A sky full of a hurricane was spelling big trouble behind them.

'I suppose Tina reads to you normally, does she?' I said.

'Tina? Tina can't read the instructions on a tin of silver polish.'

'Oh really?'

'Bless her.'

'Bless her.'

'No, Mr Parkinson reads to me.'

'Mr Parkinson.'

'He's been doing odd jobs for me for years, cleans the windows, fixes leaking taps.'

All right! A three-way split. I could cope with that. I dived into *The Wind Calls his Name* with gusto, throwing my arms about to bring the story to life.

On page four Mrs Chester fell asleep. I kept reading, but now I was taking stock, valuing the place. That landscape above the fireplace wasn't a Turner but it must have been worth a few bob. That chest was the kind of thing you'd see with a £300 tag in any antique shop. And that screen looked

Chinese. I noticed a display corner cabinet containing a collection of pieces. Quietly I got up and peered inside: an antique snuff box, some miniatures, a shelf of toby jugs and assorted silverware.

On the other side of the room, looking as fragile as Mrs Chester herself, was a beautiful clock covered in gold leaf or something, and with a porcelain face on which was painted a detailed scene from mythology – Cupid with his arrows, about to strike an unwitting couple. All around the room, in every alcove, on every surface, was something equally valuable and breakable. Even the rug beneath my feet was collectable.

I jumped as Mrs Chester grunted and I hurried back to her chair. She wasn't awake. In fact, on inspection, she didn't even seem to be breathing. I watched her closely. Her chest wasn't rising, her face was frozen, her mouth open. Her skin seemed relaxed for the first time since I'd met her. My eyes were caught by the size of the stones in her necklace.

I didn't hear the back door open. I just heard a voice, 'Hello. It's me,' and into the room came Fiona. The scene before her must have been confusing. Her dead mother upright in a chair, and, leaning over her, in his stocking feet, admiring the old bird's jewellery, was the dirty-trousered gardener. Fiona stood nonplussed, undecided whether to go out and come back in again, or call the police.

'Mother?' she said.

Mrs Chester didn't move.

'Mother!' she yelled, and Mrs Chester woke with a jump, frightening the life out of me.

'Where?' was the first thing she said.

'What?' said Fiona.

'Who?' said Mrs Chester.

'It's me,' said Fiona.

I backed out of the room and tiptoed back into the garden, where I felt safe.

What I was doing in the house was never spoken about. But from then on Fiona, Philip and Robert began to visit their mother more frequently. Each time I called during the next month one of them was always there, sitting with her, talking to her, reading or cooking for her. I rarely had dealings with her again, only occasionally saw her by the window, sitting in her armchair, wrapped in a shawl.

One morning my coffee was brought to me by a woman I'd never even seen before.

'I'm Tina,' she announced.

I wanted to put my arm on her shoulder, commiserate. I said, 'It's a shame, isn't it.'

'Pardon.'

'I know what you're going through.'

'Pardon.'

'Nothing.'

Then a few weeks later Fiona came down the garden path to me. She stood hovering for a moment, asking questions about plants, but not bothering to listen to the answers. Then she said, 'I have to tell you something, about my mother . . . she's moving.'

'Where to?'

'She's going into a residential home where she can be looked after properly. It's her decision.'

She looked pleased with herself. 'We're putting the house on the market, so I'd be grateful if you could . . . you know.'

'What?'

'Make the garden as tidy as possible.'

The sale of the house meant my job came to an end, of

course. On my last day I asked Fiona if I could say goodbye to her mother. She couldn't say no.

Mrs Chester seemed to have deteriorated. She had red eyes and cracked lips. She took my hand and shook it gently. Then whispered, as though she didn't want the children to hear, 'I won't forget you.'

But she did.

I suggested to Dick there was a sketch in the story, but he said no. 'It's wasted in a sketch. It's a movie. A gardener, played by John Travolta, murders everyone in his way to gain the inheritance. A story of lust, greed and . . .'

'. . . delphiniums.'

'Exactly. Hang onto it until we get to Hollywood.'

Hollywood seemed far off, but, even as we spoke, it was getting ever so slightly nearer. A letter from the BBC was working its way to my address. It came the next morning, the familiar BBC logo in the top left corner of the envelope. These letters invariably contained disappointing news, but they still made my heart quicken whenever they arrived. I propped it up against the salt and pepper while I ate my toast.

'What's that?' mumbled Neil.

'It's a rejection from the BBC for our outsize-shoe shop sketch.'

Neil looked at me very seriously. 'You know, you could benefit from some meditation. It would help you think more positively. I meditate three times a week and my glass is always half full, never half empty.'

'What do you think it says then?'

He looked at the letter. 'I think it's a rejection as well.'

I phoned Dick to open it together. This was a partnership. 'Are you ready?'

'Ready.'

'Ready?'

'I said I was ready!'

The letter wasn't a rejection. Not exactly a rejection, anyway. It was another message from Dave Allen's script editor. He wrote, 'Guess what, someone in the office has come up with a sketch identical to yours set in an outsize-shoe shop. Hard to believe, isn't it?'

There was a silence until Dick said, 'That's hard to believe.'

I found it hard to believe as well. But the script editor went on to say there was one of the lines that he liked, and he suggested we went in to discuss it.

'Which one of our lines?' asked Dick.

'He doesn't say.'

'We've sent him hundreds of lines.'

'Well he only likes one of them.'

Later that morning I phoned the script editor. He said, 'Come in on Tuesday. Dave's in on Tuesday.'

'Dave?'

'Dave Allen.'

We were going to meet Dave Allen. This was the biggest break we had had in seven months of writing. That evening I met Dick in the Black Lion. We sat with smug grins. We weren't exactly tasting success but surely we could smell the stuff.

'Look around you,' said Dick.

I looked around and saw the barmaid scratching her eczema; a thin man standing at the bar dropping crisps into his fat dog's gob; a young couple at the fruit machine, she nibbling his ear as he fed his wages into the slot; hanging limply from the chandelier was a lone Christmas decoration that no member of staff could be bothered to take a stepladder to. The Black Lion could easily have been the least inspiring pub in North-west London.

'Look around you and remember what you see,' Dick went on, 'because from here on everything changes.'

17

UNCLE NIGEL

For eight months I had criss-crossed Hampstead Heath on my way from job to job. I'd cycled across it in all weathers, witnessed it in all moods. I'd seen spring arrive and the great chestnut trees become beacons of red and white. I'd sheltered from thunderstorms that turned the tracks into bogs. I'd seen the grassy slopes mature into summer meadows.

I'd caught lovers giggling in the rhododendrons. I'd passed groups of students gathered around guitars; watched model aircraft soaring over Parliament Hill; and I'd seen the gardens at Kenwood bloom, and the stage appear on the lake in front of the house for the summer concerts where you brought your champagne supper and grooved along to Bach.

I'd seen the merry-go-rounds and hook-a-duck stalls go up on bank holiday weekends and turn the north-west corner of the Heath into a funfair: you came through the trees and were met by a wall of generators, loud music and screams, and kids walking round with goldfish in plastic bags. It was all there one day and gone the next.

I'd heard the splash of the women's-only swimming pool, and the rustle in the undergrowth as the homosexual prostitutes stuck their heads out and propositioned you. And I'd daily passed that bloke who did yoga from nine to ten every morning, while his dog waited patiently, looking embarrassed, trying not to belong to him.

I'd got to know the joggers who padded their lonely circuit day and night, all shapes and ages. Some would pass with an energy-saving little wave, others would stop and talk about anything they could think of as long as it meant a breather.

I'd also got to know some lads who played football on a corner of the Heath down towards Golders Green. On one occasion they asked me to play to make up numbers and I'd become involved in a regular weekly game, followed by a pint in the Old Bull and Bush.

I'd *not* got to know the fishermen who sat on boxes by the ponds and spent hours in silent retreat, meditating on life and fish, but mainly fish. I was always polite and even chatty, because I was determined that, one day before I moved out of London, I would get a smile and a greeting from one of them instead of a grunt and a curled lip.

And then there was the most ubiquitous group of all, the dog-walkers, the hundreds of people who took their charges out for their daily exercise. All sorts of people, all sorts of dogs; some walked by staff, some trotting obediently by their master's side, others bounding away to bite the heads off ducks. The Heath seemed to belong to London dogs more than to the humans.

I'd cycled across it in the twilight when the air was cool, and far below the city lay in a sepia smog. I'd walked across it on a moonlit summer's night, when there seemed to be just as many people as during the day, plus a few vampires. I'd even slept on the Heath, after a late party somewhere, when there was no point in going home. I made it up to Hampstead, kipped down under a tree for a couple of hours, then went to work.

Now it was autumn and conkers rolled down the paths, and the Heath had another use: it was the place I strolled round while I tested Helen on her fourteen times table.

She had decided to go for a job as a croupier. It meant she would have to work nights. It meant she would have to wear nail varnish. It also meant that she needed to know her times tables up to twenty.

'Sixteen seventeens?'

'Two hundred and . . . sixty-two.'

'Wrong. Two hundred and seventy-two. Why are you going for a job like this anyway?'

'I'm sick of scrubbing the rings off other people's baths. I want more respect.'

A jogger who could have been Michael Palin ran past us. 'You want more respect so you're going for a job where they pay you less, and you have to wear low-cut dresses so dirty old men can lech at you.'

'I get to use my brain.'

A juggler stood on one leg on the sports field, throwing cooking utensils into the air.

'Thirteen fourteens?'

'A hundred and seventy-eight.'

'Wrong. A hundred and eighty-two.'

The Heath was heavily populated with geese now. They bickered with each other on the model-boat lake, then took off and flew in squadrons over the slopes to arrive back in the same place. Waste of time really.

'Nineteen thirteens?'

'Two hundred and fifty-two.'

'Wrong. Two hundred and forty-seven.'

'You only ask the hard ones,' she yelled.

'All right. Three threes.'

'Nine.'

'Very good.'

She started to sulk. She'd never learn the tables in time for the interview. When we got to Swains Lane she jumped on a bus to Archway in a rotten mood. I watched her climb upstairs and sit by a window and scowl. I preferred her as a cleaner.

There was plenty of work for me now that leaves were falling. Gathering them up was all I seemed to do. It was good mindless work. I just had to remember each client had a different relationship with their leaves. Mrs Lavenham, for example, didn't mind them on her lawn but didn't want one single culprit left on her beds. 'They attract slugs!' she said, with the kind of distaste I didn't think she was capable of. Slugs were the one creature she couldn't abide. She fed and watered everything else that came into her garden, but slugs must have offended her when she was a child, because she showed them no mercy. She would pick them off the beds and squash them in her fingers, a particularly unpleasant habit for a woman with a voice so sweet she could have read the *One O'Clock News*.

Annie Kendal, on the other hand, wanted me to rake all the leaves up, but not dispose of them. She wanted her toddler, Desmond, to be able to go kicking them all over the place. For him this was the most fun you could have outside an ice-cream cone in the face, although it did make for an odd morning's work for me. I'd rake the leaves up, then sit and have a coffee while the little tyke kicked them all into the air, and then I'd spend the rest of the morning raking them all up again.

Major Chesney liked his garden completely leaf-free. He didn't even want them on a compost heap. He wanted them raked up and then tied up in a black plastic bag and put out for the dustmen. For a man who may well have seen action on Normandy beaches he seemed unusually frightened of dustmen. He was worried they would discover he was putting out garden rubbish and victimise him, so he went to great lengths to conceal the leaves amongst household rubbish, mixing in potato peelings and tin cans. 'You don't want the dustman as you enemy,' he said. 'Tricky customer, Johnny Dustman.'

'It's compost time!' was Nugent's response to autumn, reacting with the sort of enthusiasm most people reserved for spring. And of course I couldn't just dump the leaves on his compost, nothing so unscientific. I had to grade them and distribute them among the different heaps. He told me, 'Friend of mine, one year, didn't mix his leaves with more substantial material, ended up with a soggy mess, ha!' and he laughed all morning at the memory.

Nugent liked to think we had become chums. He liked to talk to me about women. He'd slap his knees and chortle in a manly way, telling me he'd never realised how much better off he'd be being single again. The truth was, of course, he pined for a partner. He always gardened with me now and I noticed that whenever he could he turned the conversation round to dating, as if I knew everything about the subject. His reckoning was: he was mid-fifties and knew about gardening; I was mid-twenties and knew about women.

'What do you reckon to blind dates?' he asked me once as we sheltered from a shower in his hut.

'I've never been on one,' I said.

'My chum Malcolm has asked me on one. He's got a lady friend and she has a friend and . . . well, I don't have to tell you how it works.'

He looked at me as if I could advise him. I just said, 'It's always good to meet new people.'

'Suppose so. Not sure how old she is, that's the trouble.'

'Can't you ask Malcolm?'

'Won't tell me.'

'Does her age matter?'

'You wouldn't want to go out on a date with a fifty-year-old, would you?'

'How old are you?'

'Oh, I'm not going through that again.'

'Through what?'

'I'm a bachelor. I want a young woman!'

We fell silent, watched the rain. I wished it would stop – I didn't want to talk to him any more; he made me uneasy. I pretended to study the roof of the shed.

'A man needs a shed,' said Nugent.

'You're right.'

He clicked his tongue. 'How about dating agencies, ever try those?'

'Nope.'

Leaves leaves leaves. A rake was the only tool I needed for weeks. Given a good-sized lawn I could spend a whole two-hour session gathering up a huge pile of leaves, and then as I left another single one would flutter down to settle gently on the grass, reminding me I'd have an identical morning's work next time.

Leaves leaves leaves. I developed raking into an art form. Lengthways was the traditional, purist's method, but, for an impressionistic effect, you could do half from the top and then half from the side. Then there was the informal, abstract pattern, or the surrealist circle, or, my favourite, the post-modern lawn which may actually have been my own creation: one rake down and one across in an ever-diminishing letter L.

Leaves leaves leaves. Then more leaves and more leaves after that. I'd never noticed how many leaves there were in the autumn before. Even after they'd been raked up, collected in doorways, blocked up drains and been pressed into kids' nature books there were a few billion left over.

'Nothing wrong with a few leaves,' said Mr Basing, who lived in Gospel Oak and had a garden with big plane trees on three sides. They weren't all his, but that didn't bother the trees and they dumped their leaves in numbers that smothered his lawn. 'Nothing wrong with a few leaves at all.' But then he handed me the rake.

What made raking Mr Basing's lawn the most satisfying of them all was that he always finished the morning with a bonfire. 'Nothing wrong with a good bonfire,' he'd say, prodding it and watching the smoke blow over to his neighbours. If anyone complained he just said, 'Oh, there's nothing wrong with a bit of smoke.'

This was his punchline. 'There's nothing wrong with a spot of rain,' he'd say, if he found me sheltering on his porch, and then he'd come out in his shirtsleeves and stand on the lawn with his arms extended to prove his point.

There was something familiar about Mr Basing. He reminded you of an uncle you hadn't seen for a long time. 'Call me Nigel,' he said, after a couple of visits, and I thought, Uncle Nigel.

He was always perfectly dressed for the occasion. When he went to the newsagent he had a special going-down-to-the-newsagent pullover. When he went off to the Heath with the dog he was always dressed in his dog-walking wind-cheater. When he was in the garden he always wore a checked shirt and flat cap. Everything was immaculately pressed. If a thing was worth doing it was worth dressing up for.

And yet, compared to other clients, it was very hard to categorise Nigel Basing. Most people I gardened for had Solicitor, Chemist, Musician, or whatever, written all over them. But Nigel was an enigma. His car said he was a salesman; his shoes said GP; his wife said airline pilot. I couldn't work him out – what he did for a living. He went to work at odd times. He wore a raincoat. He carried a briefcase, but his wife didn't stand on the doorstep and kiss him goodbye. He liked to hum as he walked down the garden path. He didn't have the golf-club tie of a bank manager. He spoke precisely, like a scientist, but . . . sometimes he went to work in jeans.

I suppose I could easily have found out – just asked him, or his wife. But that wasn't the game.

I continued to rake his leaves and he continued to watch them burn, leaning on his fork in his Viyella shirt with cuffs turned over twice to halfway between the wrist and elbow, a raffish scarf round his neck, a poet's scarf perhaps? It was no good. I couldn't read the clues, and at the end of one session I said to him, 'Nigel, I don't wish to be nosy, but what do you do for a living?'

He looked at me for a moment, wondering if he'd heard me correctly. 'Bit of this, bit of that,' he joked.

'I just wondered . . .'

'None of your damn business.'

Our meeting with Dave Allen kept being postponed. The script editor would phone up and say, 'Don't come in today.

It's not a good idea,' as if Dave was in a bad mood and didn't want to answer questions from trainee writers.

Helen's career had become equally problematic. She had been asked back to an audition. It was for a part in a soap opera that would give her a job for six months and a load of money. But the audition was on the same day as her interview for the croupier job. Now she was walking across the Heath learning a speech from *Under Milk Wood* as well as her times tables.

'A soap opera?'

'That's right.'

'Do you think *Under Milk Wood* is the sort of thing they want to hear?'

'They said something I liked.'

'Yes but . . .'

'But what?'

'You're too talented for a silly soap.'

'It's good.'

'It's rubbish.'

'First my cleaning job and now my acting. You're being judgemental.'

'You're right.'

'"Oh, the Spring whinny and . . . and . . ."'

'"Morning moo."'

'I know!'

We walked towards Kenwood, wading through leaves. I had an urge to start raking them up into neat little piles.

In the converted coach house that was the Kenwood café we were the only people having tea. Helen closed *Under Milk Wood* and switched to her seventeen times table. Her voice echoed round the stone walls. 'Twelve seventeens are two hundred and four. Thirteen seventeens are two hundred and twenty-one.'

She said her boyfriend was fed up with her going round the house reciting things. I was beginning to understand how he felt, the difference being he lived with her and I didn't, but would have liked to.

But it did mean that I was becoming expert in my times tables as well. This was a great way to annoy Neil. He couldn't stand me knowing something that he didn't. 'Fourteen nineteens,' I'd say in his face, and his lip would quiver as he fought to work it out before I said, 'Time's up. Two hundred and sixty-six.'

'Knowing that is absolutely no use to anyone,' he said.

'Yes it is.'

'You're a gardener.'

'It's useful if you're planting seeds and you've got fourteen rows and you want to plant nineteen seeds in each and you want to know how many to buy.'

'I know my tables,' said Mandy.

'Sure,' said Neil.

'Thirteen times sixteen?' I asked her.

'Two hundred and eight,' she said.

'Correct.'

Neil sat up. 'That was a guess!'

'Fifteen times nineteen?'

'Two hundred and eighty-five,' she said without hesitation.

Both Neil and I were stunned.

'I do have an IQ of one hundred and thirty-eight,' she said. 'I could join Mensa.'

'They don't allow hairdressers into Mensa,' said Neil, and ran into the bathroom.

The clocks went back. The leaves eased off. Some kids put a guy on the street by the Royal Free Hospital and asked for money. '50p for the guy,' one of the lads called to me.

I was staggered. '50p. That's a bit steep.'

'This is Hampstead!'

Uncle Nigel was beginning to annoy me. I saw him in Hampstead Village once, striding along, the way he did, talking to himself, head up but in his own world. I decided to follow him; maybe he worked locally. I watched him go into the newsagent and come out with a copy of the *Radio Times*. Then he went to the off-licence, then he went to the library. He came out with two books. Then he went home. Hmm.

I went to rake up the final leaves at his house one afternoon and he came out, heading off somewhere, wearing old suede shoes and leather gloves. He sniffed the chill in air: 'Nothing wrong with a chill in the air,' he said, and blew a cloud. Then he walked down the path and all but jumped over the garden gate. How could he be so damn jolly, so smug? I felt irritation rising in me. He had a secret and I wanted to know it.

His wife was in and I asked if I could use the toilet.

'Of course,' she said, then looked at my feet. I took my shoes off. She still looked at my feet. I took my socks off.

She led me through the house. My eyes were everywhere: the prints on the wall, the photos on the mantelpiece. Was that a Member of the Institute of Chartered Surveyors certificate on the wall next to the bay window?

She showed me to the downstairs cloakroom. The walls were covered with framed photographs: classes at school, sports teams, holiday snaps. But they were all from days in the 1940s and '50s when both Basings were youngsters. There was one of Northampton Grammar 1951, a bunch of boys standing in rows. I searched it for Nigel but couldn't recognise him. There was a picture of a football team, and there he was, more hair, less tummy, but as immaculately turned out as ever: polished boots, double-knotted laces, hair combed and brilliantined. You couldn't imagine Nigel ever getting his knees dirty, even at football.

In all this memorabilia I thought there had to be a clue to what he had become in life. But no, I could find nothing. I rifled through the magazines in the rack hoping to find *Magic and Magicians* monthly or something that would be a giveaway, but it was full of *Cosmopolitan* and *Country Life*. I even searched the cabinet under the sink. This was the only real shock in the room. Instead of disinfectant and spare toilet rolls it contained a large number of tins of rice pudding. This should have told me something about the Basings, but I couldn't think what.

Mrs Basing was by the front door as I came out, there to check I didn't leave a crumb of dirt on her mat as I put my socks and shoes back on. I decided on a trick question. 'So. It must be hard work for your husband being a politician?'

'Isn't that funny?' she said.

'What?'

'What?'

'What's funny?'

'Lots of people think he's a politician.'

I laughed. 'So what is he then?'

'Oh, he's not a politician.'

'But . . .'

'Here he comes now.'

There was Uncle Nigel striding down the garden path. He beamed at his wife; he beamed at me. I felt defeated. I wanted to punch him on the nose.

The day of Helen's job interview and her audition came. At the casino she got all her times-table questions wrong, and yet the manager still offered her the job. She declined it, however. She said, 'He wore big gold rings, and I could never have worked in a place with a carpet like that.'

Then in the afternoon she went for her second audition for the soap opera. She said she performed very well. She read her piece from *Under Milk Wood* with conviction and a soft Welsh accent, but she didn't get the part.

She was angry when I saw her. She said, 'It was because of my ears.'

'What's wrong with your ears?'

'They're big.'

'No they're not.'

'You're just saying that.'

'Your ears are not big!' I looked closely at her ears. Actually, they were a *bit* big.

'It's a sad day when you can't get a job because your ears are too big,' she said.

When the episode she auditioned for was to be aired she told me I had to watch and tell her what I thought of the actor who got the job in her place. Her character was Paula who worked behind the reception at the hotel.

I made Neil watch it with me, and Mandy. We sat quietly and listened to every word. I wondered if I'd been a gardener too long when I started to notice the pot plants in the hotel reception and could name them all.

'The girl behind the reception is the one we need to be watching,' I told them.

But I never saw the girl behind reception. I never saw anyone from the moment a man in a brown suit came into shot and started ordering the staff about in a managerial but very familiar way. It was Uncle Nigel.

My first reaction was: what the hell is Nigel Basing doing on my television? Then I realised he hadn't wandered onto the set; he was supposed to be there. He was a character in the show. He was an actor in a soap opera. That was what he did.

The date to meet Dave Allen was rearranged for November the Fifth. It seemed fitting that fireworks should go off all around town on the day our career was launched.

I woke that morning with an ivy rash all over my arms that made me scratch and squirm. The only thing that soothed it was TCP, which I splashed on. No-one sat near me on the tube.

I'd arranged to meet Dick at the BBC reception. This time he wore a white jacket that would have looked the part in a jazz club.

'You got it from the charity shop, didn't you?' I said.

'Of course I got it from the bloody charity shop.' He seemed put out by the idea that he might have bought clothes anywhere else.

We took the lift up to the fourth floor again, to the script editor's office. 'I think we should lighten up a bit this time,' said Dick.

'You're right'

'Make him think we're normal people.'

'But with a sharp observational kind of wit.'

'Yeah.'

Dick sniffed me. 'You smell like an old people's home.'

The script editor was very wary of us. He chewed his pen and didn't get up from behind his desk. I sat as far away from him as I could.

'So which line of ours did Dave Allen like?' asked Dick.

'The one about the guy who wins the Nobel Prize for doorknockers.'

We had never written a line about the Nobel Prize for doorknockers, although I wished we had.

'That's one of my favourites as well,' said Dick. 'It treads that line between humour and . . . and . . .'

The script editor waited, wondering what he was going to say.

'Humour and . . .' Dick looked at his watch.

The script editor looked at his watch. 'Let's go and meet Dave,' he said.

We jumped up and followed him down the corridor to another office. And there was Dave Allen, in real life, standing by the window clutching files, speaking to his director and producer. We were introduced as two lads who were writing interesting material. Dave nodded wisely. He shook my hand.

'Hard hands,' he said.

'I'm a gardener.'

He nodded wisely again.

The producer and director said that they liked the Nobel Prize and doorknocker line, but couldn't use it as it was. Maybe we could develop it.

'It needs more texture,' said the director.

'Look at the tone,' said the producer.

Then Dave Allen had to go. But as he left he turned to me, and said, 'A gardener?'

'That's right.'

'Tell me . . .'

'Yes?'

'What's the best time of year to plant a leylandii?'

Dick and I glanced at each other. He looked tense, not having a clue what a leylandii was. I looked pale, not because I didn't know what a leylandii was, I did, but I had no idea when you were supposed to plant the things.

I didn't hesitate. I said, 'September . . .'

'September?' said Dave.

'September. Second half of the month.'

'Right.'

'Say, the 25th.'

'The 25th.'

'In the evening. Six o'clockish.'

'Thanks.'

'You're welcome.'

And he was gone.

And we never heard from Dave Allen or his script editor ever again.

WINTER

18

THE VIRGIN MARY

Now it was dark by five o'clock. Frosts hardened the Heath. The ponds became icy. Bernie looked to Christmas to give his garden centre the boost it needed. He filled his shop with gnomes and decorated with tinsel. He put signs up in the window suggesting shears – the perfect present for him; or a trug basket – perfect for her.

Lawns no longer needed cutting, nor beds weeding. The leaves were gone, perennials had been cut back. Nature began to shut down, and, one by one, clients let me go, asking me to return in the spring. All summer I had wondered why I seemed to be the only jobbing gardener in North London. Now I knew why: the others had all starved the previous winter.

Gaps appeared in my schedule. Money disappeared from my bank account. I asked Neil for time to pay the rent. He put his hands on my shoulders and said, 'I am thou, thou art I, he is ours, we both are his.'

'I'll take that as a yes.'

Enough people kept me on to stop me from going completely under. Mrs Lavenham, for instance, wouldn't have dreamed of laying me off. 'Lots to do in the winter,' she said. She was a job-creation scheme all by herself. She had me aerating her lawn. She instructed me to dig a new bed by the beech hedge where she wanted to put bulbs. We planted a pear tree together. Any time there was nothing obvious to do she'd hand me a pot of creosote and a big brush, and point me at the fence, saying, 'It's good fun, creosoting, I always think.'

She was particularly excited lately because she was organising a local Gardeners' Question Time. It was a fund-raiser to be held at the beginning of December, and she was going to be on the panel along with some other notable local gardeners. 'Leslie Dunwoody is coming,' she said with glee. 'He wrote a whole book on north-facing borders. The man's a hoot!' She gave me an invite and then asked if I would give flyers to all the people I gardened for. She wanted a good turnout. 'Glass of mulled wine and mince pie included in the ticket price,' she enthused.

'Leave it with me,' I said. 'I'll have the place packed out.' It was the least I could do. She'd been so good to me. She felt like family.

'Would you like some pinks for your garden?' she asked as I was leaving.

I accepted them gratefully.

'I'd like to see your garden one day,' she said.

'Of course,' I gushed. 'You must.'

She'd got this idea from somewhere that I lived on an estate with fountains and orchards, and borders that were herbaceousness itself, not to mention my camomile lawn and bountiful vegetable patch. It was an image I rather liked and so I never corrected her, never told her that

246

the most fragrant thing in my garden was the wheelie bin.

She handed me the pinks in a plastic bag and I did what I did with all the flowers she or anyone else gave me, I took them round to Joan Peek and her son Jamie in Crouch End. Over the summer I'd stocked her little garden so well with lifted and donated flowers that its two beds were now stuffed. It was the garden I knew best of all — I'd started it from an empty bed — and I think it was my favourite as well, because Joan and Jamie got so much fun out of such a small patch. I liked to think it had had a therapeutic effect on them. They didn't scream as much. They would often be out there watering plants when I arrived. Jamie had his toys spread about; Joan would sit out on a kitchen chair sunning her legs. The garden had improved their life.

Joan was as grateful as she ever was when I handed her the pinks, and then when I gave her the Gardeners' Question Time flyer I could see her on the edge of tears again. I think she might have been about to hug me, but Jamie drove his truck over her foot and the moment was gone.

'Is it formal?' she asked. 'I've nothing to wear.'

'Come as you are.'

'And I'll need a babysitter.'

'Bring him along. The more the merrier.'

Before I left she said, 'Will you call again next week? We've got something for you.'

'OK.'

'It's a Christmas present,' said Jamie, blowing the secret, and then blowing a raspberry.

I was grateful for any work anyone could give me, even Walters, the man with the model village in his garden and the huge collection of pesticides. He asked if I was free on November 30th. I told him I was and he said, 'Good. Nine o'clock on the dot.'

I knew it would be nothing to do with gardening, it never was with him. He probably wanted his ornamental wind-mills oiled or his pixies painted. Maybe an electric fence around his plot for extra security.

But I could never have guessed the job he had for me. 'He's up in the roof,' his wife said, when I presented myself as arranged, and she led me upstairs to the loft hatch. Above me, Walters appeared, strewn with cobwebs. 'Catch this,' he yelled and dropped a box of fairy lights on top of me.

Other bags and boxes came out, and we carried them all out into the garage where he carefully unwrapped them to reveal his impressive collection of Christmas decorations, indoor and out. 'I like to give the Close a good display,' he said. 'They've come to expect it over the years.'

The front of the house was about to be turned into Santa's grotto. We started with a loop of lights that linked the two large conifers. 'Some people kick up a fuss, of course,' said Walters. 'But I don't think the complaints of the few should spoil the pleasure of the majority. Do you?'

'No,' I said. But I needed the work.

He put his ladders up against the house, and I passed him up strings of lights which he hooked around the windows. 'These flash on and off,' he said proudly.

Another loop was fixed to the gutters. 'Green and red,' said Walters, 'my favourite colours,' and when I stood back I could see they spelt out NOEL.

All this seemed so unlike Walters. I would have guessed Scrooge was his role model, but here he was with his eyes lit up like a little boy's. Christmas was something very special for him.

We secured plastic snowmen to the gateposts at the end of the drive. Battery-powered lanterns were suspended on hooks in the front rockery. A crib the size of a bus shelter, and backlit, became a nativity scene in the centre of the lawn, the Holy Family clearly visible from the road. If he'd put that up in a garden on my street there'd have been a real family sleeping in it by morning.

'Now for the pièce de résistance,' said Walters, as he emerged from the garage clutching a roof ladder.

'You're not going up on the roof?' I said.

'No I'm not,' he said. 'Mrs Walters is.'

Mrs Walters was busy spraying all the inside windows with aerosol snow, but when Walters called her she came out dressed in dungarees and yellow gloves. 'Off you go dear,' said Walters, and he handed her one end of a length of lights.

'I don't enjoy this bit,' he said quietly, as he watched her climb to the gutter, then hook the roof ladder onto the ridge and transfer herself. 'She's never fallen yet, but . . . there's always a first time.'

She was a nimble woman, was Mrs Walters. She moved across the roof like a puma with a perm. She attached each end of the string of lights to the chimney stacks and then secured the middle to the ridge. 'That's the ticket,' said Walters, sipping his morning coffee.

Then she let the lights unravel, and they fell across the tiles to reveal a design which I couldn't make out just yet, but I was more concerned with Mrs Walters's trailing foot as it tried to find the top rung of the ladder and begin a descent. She made contact and shinned down to earth like a fireman. 'She's a plucky girl,' said Walters.

Now he plugged in the extension cord and he held his wife's hand as they stood back and turned on the display. They were celebrities switching on their own Oxford Street lights. And there it was, a sleigh with a sack of presents in the back, pulled by a red-nosed reindeer flying across the roof of the house, and ridden by a waving Santa. I was left open-mouthed. Walters had a tear in his eye. 'Don't you love Christmas?' he said.

I went to see all the clients I had gardened for over the previous eight months and gave each of them a flyer to Mrs Lavenham's Question Time, then suggested I should do for them all the winter jobs I was doing for her, but they looked at me as if I was mad. There was nothing growing in the gardens; why couldn't I hibernate like everything else? I swept a few drives, and a few people told me I could tidy up the shed. I must have spent most of November in one shed or another, among balls of green string and ancient bottles of liquid derris.

Kenneth the composer didn't have a shed, but he was in the process of doing something about that. He asked me to come round one morning and he very proudly showed me the new model he had just bought. 'An early Christmas present to myself,' he said.

He called it a shed but the word didn't really do it justice; it was more like a ski lodge at the bottom of his garden. 'It's Norwegian,' he said. 'Came on a big truck. They brought it down the garden on a forklift. Only took ten minutes.' He was very pleased with it.

He wanted me to put shelves up. He planned to have seed trays spread about, and to hang tools on the wall. He wanted spiders everywhere and piles of flower pots: 'Not the plastic sort, ceramic.'

It was a good idea, but, of course, he couldn't go through with it. I put the shelves up as asked, but he used them to display photos and ornaments rather than slug pellets. He had a nice stereo system in there by the next time I called, and an easy chair where he sat huddled in an overcoat, humming to himself. 'I like working in here,' he said. 'It's a garret. I wrote my first jingle in a garret.'

How pleasant for him. He was so wealthy he was able to recreate the days when he was impoverished, except now, if he got fed up with it, he just strode across the lawn into his big house and opened a bottle of Chablis. I said to him, 'Did you have a part-time job when you started out, just to keep you going?'

'Of course I did. I was music teacher to an Italian duke's children. I lived in a palazzo in Tuscany.'

'Must have been hell.'

Kenneth lived round the corner from the Walters and I asked him if he'd seen the Christmas lights. He laughed and laughed.

'What's funny?'

'Haven't you heard? He's had his Virgin Mary stolen. It's not funny really.'

It was true. Poor Walters. He was inconsolable. 'What kind of person would do a thing like that?' he said.

The crib was indeed one parent short. The infant was motherless. Joseph had been powerless to protect his wife.

'When did it happen?' I asked.

'I don't know. Mrs Walters noticed it when she came out to get the milk.'

He was genuinely upset. Whoever did it can only have been having a joke, but it was in pretty bad taste.

'They ignored the sheep, you'll notice, and the shepherds. They knew what they were looking for. They went straight for the Mother of God. It's blasphemy!'

He suspected everyone: all his neighbours, the window

cleaner, the postman. 'Twenty-two years I've been putting up these decorations and nothing like this has ever happened. Mrs Walters has had to take a pill.'

He was knocking together a sign, red letters on a white background, very Christmassy. It read: 'Will the person who stole the Virgin Mary please put her back.' He nailed it to a post and stuck it in the front bed. Then he went indoors and took up a position in the window. I don't think he was armed.

Where do you look for a three-foot-high Virgin Mary? No place sprang to mind. Maybe it would be found by a dog under a bush on the Heath, in the way Pickles found the Jules Rimet trophy in 1966. Or maybe it would disappear for good, like Shergar. I told Walters he should go to the police, but he took a step back at the very idea, as if the last thing he wanted was the police snooping round his house.

Soon, though, there was a development in the case. When I saw Walters again he took me into his garage, as if this was the only place we could talk safely, and he pulled a note out of his pocket. 'Came this morning.'

'What is it?'

'A ransom demand.'

I laughed, but there it was written in big letters across a page of tabloid newspaper. Walters read it out. '£100 or Mary gets it!'

It was a joke, but Walters was taking it very seriously. He showed me the envelope; it had a first-class stamp and an E17 postmark.

'Outsiders,' said Walters. 'Probably foreigners, funda-mentalists with no respect for Christian beliefs. Well I'm sorry, I'm not giving in to their demands. You can't nego-tiate with these people, it just encourages them.'

But the note also had a muddy thumbprint in the middle

of it, and the circle of a glass stain across the bottom. And the newspaper was the *Daily Star*.

I knew who the jokers were.

Powerflowers didn't seem to have been as badly affected as I was by the end of the season. They still prowled the same patch, hanging out of their cab like chimps. Like me they planned to survive the closed season by diversifying. They built driveways and patios; they put up carports and fences. They revved their chainsaws and tried to look butch.

I saw their van one morning parked across the road from Major Chesney. The major had asked me to come round to do an inventory on his plants.

'A what?' I'd said.

'An inventory.'

'You mean . . . you want me to count them?'

'Precisely.'

'Why?'

'It's that time of year.'

Well of course it was. It was December, the time of year when everyone is out in their garden counting their plants.

I was in the front, adding up his roses, while Power-flowers spent the morning lugging barrowfuls of stone out of their truck to the back of the house where they were working. It was time to confront them again. I marched over to Don. He had bloodshot eyes and a fresh shaving cut.

I came straight to the point. 'Would you know anything about a model of the Virgin Mary that's gone missing from a garden off Hampstead Lane?'

He looked at me shiftily, took out his tobacco tin and said, 'Are you taking the piss?'

'One of the people I garden for has had a model of the

Virgin Mary stolen from his nativity scene. I wondered if you knew anything about it.'

He rolled a lumpy cigarette and licked the end of it. 'There's only one thing I know.'

'What's that?'

'It's lunchtime, and I'm going to the pub.' And as he said the word pub his gang appeared in a flash and they all piled in the van and were gone. Maybe they were annoyed that they were the only people I hadn't asked to the charity Gardeners' Question Time.

The house where they were working looked vacant – bare walls and floors, no curtains. It looked as if it had just been extensively renovated – knocked through and opened out. The garage had been left open and I was able to go round to the back where Powerflowers were working. They had been called in to build a garden path and some steps leading down to the lawn. The plot was a mess, strewn with debris, but soon they would fire up their artillery and the wilderness would be tamed.

I kicked around the site, the rubble and the pork-pie wrappers. I don't know what I was hoping to find, but I was convinced this lot had stolen the statue. I could just see them guffawing in the pub, writing the ransom note on a newspaper, placing an incriminating glass at the bottom, posting it when they got home.

There was no evidence, though, no holy feet sticking out from under a tarpaulin. I felt powerless. I knocked over a box of nails on purpose. When I saw a radio on the step I took the back off and removed the batteries, and pocketed them. Silly thing to do, but I felt better.

As I left a neighbour saw me. I froze, guilt written all over me. 'What are you doing?' he said.

'I'm going to the pub. What d'you think I'm doing?'

*   *   *

Walters began to accept that he wasn't going to see the Virgin Mary again, and he was probably right. 'One of those things,' he said, although it was clear Christmas had been spoilt for ever, and, unfortunately, this episode just reinforced his belief that the nation was in freefall and he was only safe in the Ruritania he had created behind his high fences.

But he was determined his seasonal display would go ahead as normal, and so he bought a replacement for the crib. A substitute Virgin now smiled down on the infant. But the scale of the newcomer was all wrong. Mary was bigger than Joseph, and the shepherds; bigger even than the Magi on their camels. She looked like a Mardi Gras version of herself, big eyes and lips. Enough to terrify the baby Jesus.

The whole saga wasn't quite over, though. The next day I called in, as promised, at Joan and Jamie's in Crouch End. I was asked to sit down, and given a cup of tea. Jamie was jumping with excitement.

Joan spoke as if she was about to hand out an award at a prizegiving. She took a deep breath and said, 'For the last six months you've been very good to me and Jamie. And, to show our gratitude for all the nice plants you've brought us, Jamie would like to give you something.'

At a nod from her Jamie ran out of the room and ran back in with a piece of artwork. He handed it to me with a face full of pride.

'This is it!' he said.

It was a drawing of the garden, in full bloom. A splash of multicoloured flowers with a big sun shining down from a perfect blue sky. There was a matchstick Jamie holding a bucket, and there was a beachball-like mum — a pile of blobs in different colours stacked on top of each other, finished with green hair.

But there was a third figure, standing among the flowers,

hat on head, a zip of a smile on his face. 'That's you,' said Jamie. 'You're in the garden.'

A lump came to my throat, damn it! And I felt the sudden urge to go down on one knee and propose to Joan, and move in and be a stepdad and be part of this little family unit; and sit outside in the patch of ex-wilderness and watch the sun go down over Alexandra Palace far into the next millennium.

'Thank you,' I said, and composed myself.

'Have you got a fridge?' Joan asked.

'Yes thanks.'

'You can stick the drawing on it.'

'Right.'

And I would have done just that, but on the way home I was cycling along Spaniards Road when the Powerflowers' van passed me in the opposite direction. They hooted at me, and Don, at the wheel, opened his window and screamed, 'Oi!'

I ignored him. I was getting used to them shouting at me from their van. But then I heard cars sounding their horns, and when I looked round I saw that Powerflowers were holding up the traffic with a three-point turn. They were turning round and coming after me.

My legs ploughed into my pedals until my tyres began to smoke. I was a streamlined beast in wellingtons and muddy corduroy as I sped along in the general direction of some-where else. A glance over my shoulder and I could see the van gaining on me. Ahead was a man on a zebra crossing, the traffic stopped for him, but I flew past him on the inside. If I'd hit him head on I wouldn't have done as much damage as Powerflowers wanted to do to me.

But I couldn't outrun them. They were two vehicles away, honking, and leaning out of their windows yelling at me to stop. There was nothing else for it: I jumped the bike up onto the pavement and just kept on going into the under-growth that bordered the Heath. Momentum carried me straight through the bushes and down a bank into long grass. I put my head down and forced a passage through a thicket, until I emerged on a path that eventually led me into the gardens of Kenwood House. They couldn't follow me here, but I didn't stop pedalling until I was far away on the other side of the ponds, where, if threatened, I could have run into Major Chesney's house and pleaded with him to unlock his gun cabinet.

It was then I realised that the plastic bag which I normally had strapped to the back of my bike had gone, and with it, Jamie's picture.

By now it was getting dark and I had a puncture. I pushed my bike home, feeling miserable. Neil said he'd fix me up with his beautiful girlfriend's almost as beautiful sister if it would make me feel better. But I had a sense things were coming to a head and there was only one secure place to be: under the duvet with a supermarket lasagne, and the headphones on listening to John Peel.

Powerflowers got me in the end, of course. In fact they got me the next day. I had just spent the morning with Nugent, digging up his dahlias, the leaves already blackened by frost. He was storing them in a greenhouse, temperature-controlled with a paraffin heater. It was warmer in there than Neil ever allowed our flat to get.

He then had me help him lay a carpet over the back bed, the one he said he wanted to reclaim. I thought this was a bit flash, carpeting your garden, but Nugent looked at me pityingly. 'Kills off the weeds, dear boy. I'm going to grow soft fruit here.' I still had a lot to learn.

I left him and headed off to Dick's pub. Our self-imposed

deadline for success was getting closer, although we didn't speak about it. God knew what we were going to do if we stopped writing.

We were turning out a dying burst of jokes. We looked for a sketch in every situation. When Dick saw one of the flyers for Mrs Lavenham's Gardeners' Question Time he demanded to know why he hadn't been invited.

'What do you want to come for?'

'Material.'

'There's no material in a charity Gardeners' Question Time.'

'There is if you know nothing about gardening and you ask stupid questions.'

'I don't want to see you there, all right?'

'I'll gatecrash it.'

I was cycling home down a back street through Kentish Town, watching the snowflakes settling on me, wondering what part of the globe Stu the Australian was on this winter's night. I didn't see the Powerflowers van loom up behind. But then it overtook me, and pulled up right in my path. I slammed on the brakes, swerved around the van, across the road and under some railway arches. They shouted at me and followed. I turned another corner, nipped under another set of arches with the van right behind me now. I turned again, but this time found myself in a dead-end street that backed onto a railway yard.

There was nothing I could do. I turned to face them. The van stopped, the engine shuddered and died. Don climbed down and moved slowly towards me. There was no-one else around; he could have chainsawed my head off and I wouldn't have been found for days. I decided to be strong and silent. If he made a move I'd pistol-whip him with my high-pressure tyre pump.

A train clattered overhead. I noticed Don had a skull and crossbones tattoo on his forearm.

The train passed. All was quiet. Don said, 'D'you want a job?'

19

JOHN LLOYD

Powerflowers wanted help with a patio they were laying at a large house in Golders Green. One of their crew had left. 'He did a bunk to Saudi,' said Don.

It wasn't gardening; it was building, but tempting nevertheless, and it would have meant a regular wage. I told Don I'd think about it, but it was going to be hard to refuse.

My writing time with Dick would have been most affected. Powerflowers wanted me at work by eight thirty, and I wouldn't have had afternoons free any more. It was everything I had spent the last eight months trying to avoid.

I explained the situation to Dick. He was very understanding. He said, 'We're packing up anyway, aren't we? We failed, let's face it. We're crap. Rubbish.'

'It's only the first week in December. We've got till Christmas.'

But the future didn't look promising. Annie Kendal was next to lay me off. 'Suppose you'll go on holiday now,' she said.

'That's right. The Seychelles.'

'Very pleasant.'

'Then I'll probably go skiing until the spring.'

'What a nice life you lead.'

Helen and I met for a tea break in the café of the Royal Free Hospital casualty department. She had taken to going there to watch the nurses. She said it was good experience for when she had an audition for a hospital drama.

I told her about Powerflowers' offer and she said, 'There are worse jobs.'

'Like what?'

We called in at the Job Centre. There was no work for gardeners or scriptwriters. She perused the engineering, office-work, and kitchen-staff notice boards for something to suit me. The very idea made me want to get on my bike and ride off into the sunset.

'I want to work outside,' I said.

'You should get a job which will give you the experience and background information you need to write something award-winning.'

Now that was a good idea.

'Here, look. Traffic warden!'

As the days grew shorter there was a sense of things drawing to a close. Mrs Lavenham was my only regular client now. After much publicity and preparation the day of her Gardeners' Question Time had finally arrived, and it promised to be the event of the season. 'All your advertising has paid off,' she told me. 'We've sold over 200 tickets.'

She was baking trays of mince pies, and mixing vats of mulled wine. 'I have one more favour to ask you,' she said.

'Anything.'

'I'm afraid Leslie Dunwoody has let us down. I need you to stand in for him.'

'I beg your pardon?'

'You'll be all right.'

She had to be joking. Me, on a Gardeners' Question Time panel? If people found out how little I really knew I'd never work again.

'I don't think that's a very good idea.'

'Nonsense.'

'No no.'

'You're a gardener.'

'Surely you can find someone else?'

'It's such short notice. And people around here know you now.'

'I'm going to my bicycle-maintenance class tonight.'

'And it's for a very good cause.'

'What cause?'

'Royal National Lifeboat Institution. My husband was in the Navy.'

And she looked at me with the kind of fearless face that she must have shown to her husband when she waved him off to war. Be brave, she was saying to me, and I knew I had no choice. If things were coming to an end, at least I'd go out with a bang.

'See you there at seven thirty then,' I said.

I went home and tried to speed-read *The Reader's Digest Complete Gardener* I'd bought at Oxfam for 10p. But I was too unsettled to concentrate. A jumble of facts spun around my head: there is little to be done with heather during July apart from weeding and renewing the peat mulch; clip your hedge for the last time in September; February is the time to order your summer-flowering Dutch iris bulbs.

Neil came in and I explained the situation to him in the hope that he could concoct some herbal remedy that would give me inner calm and carry me through the evening on a wave of serenity, or alternatively knock me out cold for twenty-four hours.

'You mean drugs,' he said.

'I mean cosmic nectar.'

He had nothing to offer me but a lift up to Hampstead.

'Why are you going to Hampstead?'

'I wouldn't miss this for anything.'

Mandy decided to come as well. She dressed up as if she was going to a movie premiere.

'All you're going to see is me making a fool of myself,' I told her.

She shrugged and glued on her false fingernails. 'Will there be TV cameras there?'

'No.'

'Press?'

'No.'

'Anybody famous?'

'No.'

'I'll never understand gardening.'

On the way up to Hampstead we passed many gardens I had worked in over the last nine months. I had built myself a little career here. It was about to fall apart, but I had no reason to feel regret. Gardening had provided me with a good living. It had kept me fit. It had kept me free.

When we got to the hall I was astonished at the number of people I knew there. Nugent met me at the door dressed in a tight T-shirt and jeans. 'Never know who you're going to meet at these affairs,' he said with a wink.

Annie Kendal waved and introduced me to her husband. 'This is Robert. He's the Overseas Sales Manager for

Pickering, Maggs, Norton, Cockbain and . . .'

'. . . and Allardyce,' said her husband, offering his hand.

Major Chesney was there, already on his third glass of mulled wine, his nose the colour of a plum.

A tug at my sleeve and there was Joan Peek. 'Where's Jamie?' I asked.

'I got my neighbour to babysit. She's just out of rehab, but beggars can't be choosers.' She was dressed in a very smart black outfit. In an instant Nugent was by my side: 'Aren't you going to introduce me to your friend?'

Bernie was also there, also wanting introductions. 'Good place to meet new customers, socialise a bit.'

I introduced him to Kenneth the composer. Bernie asked him, 'So who's your main influence?'

'Schubert,' said Kenneth. 'And who's your main influence?'

No-one had ever asked Bernie that before. 'Fisons, I suppose,' he said. 'Maybe Black and Decker.'

Lady Brignal put in an appearance. 'I shall always support the RNLI. We have a cruiser at Falmouth.' And Helen was with her. 'I want you to ask me a really easy question,' I said to her. 'Or I'm doomed.'

Walters was there with his wife. 'Mrs Walters wouldn't dream of missing a local event,' he said. I introduced them to Sweeney, the pensioner activist, a man with no small talk. 'I want you to come on a march on Saturday?' he said to them. 'Pensioners against privatisation.' Walters stepped in front of his wife as if he was protecting her from a flasher.

I made my way to the front where Mrs Lavenham was gathering the other panellists together. In quick succession I was introduced to three people whose names I immediately forgot: a woman wearing a fur stole and false eyelashes who looked as though the nearest she'd ever been to a garden was the restaurant at Kew; then, by contrast, a man who looked as though he'd come straight from the garden and brought half of it along with him embedded in his fingernails; and finally a man who shook my hand robustly and said, 'I'm an air-traffic controller. What do you do?'

'He's a gardener,' said Mrs Lavenham, which made them all sit up.

Having impressed my panel mates so easily, now was really the time to sneak out and spend the rest of the evening in the Freemason's Arms, but I could feel destiny pushing me towards my chair on the platform. Last spring I had lied and tricked my way into this job and now I was going to pay my dues, in humiliation.

Mrs Lavenham clapped her hands and brought the room to attention. She welcomed the audience, commenting on how such a large turnout could only point to the great interest and care with which local residents treated their gardens, and if tonight contributed in any way towards a better crop next year – as well as helping to buy a new lifeboat – then it would all be worthwhile. Then she introduced the panel. The man with dirty fingernails had recently returned from an orchid-hunting trip to South America. The woman in the fur stole turned out to be an authority on Victorian plants. The air-traffic controller had won second prize in some category at Chelsea. I was introduced as someone who needed no introduction. Helen gave a cheer. Annie Kendal gave a little wave. Nugent guffawed. I sat smiling like a ventriloquist's dummy.

'So can we have the first question,' said Mrs Lavenham, and Major Chesney put his hand up: 'Any more mince pies?'

I could have answered that one, or taken a guess anyway, but a pie was passed to him without comment, and the first question proper came. It concerned sweet peas, and whether the panel had any tips on the best way to grow them. Mrs

Lavenham fielded this to the orchid expert, who nodded thoughtfully and then answered in a language that I certainly didn't understand, and I wondered if anyone in the audience did either. He used two Latin words for every English one, and made a joke which was probably the only sweet-pea joke in existence. He spoke for about five minutes after which the audience clapped politely, although the woman who had asked the question, and sat listening throughout with her pen poised to take notes, was left with a blank sheet of paper, looking round herself, wondering if she'd walked into the wrong event.

The next question concerned poinsettias, and how to keep them growing and healthy throughout the festive season. Mrs Lavenham gave this one to the authority on Victorian plants, who launched into a history of the poinsettia, and told a story of the time in 1956 when she went to Lapland for Christmas to stay with a member of the Norwegian royal family who took her out on a reindeer hunt, and they got caught in a blizzard and had to ski home and only made it back to the castle thanks to some friendly Lapps who took them into their camp and gave them warm blood and biscuits to revive them, and, while the aurora borealis turned the heavens green and red, the thing that really caught her eye was what wonderful poinsettias the Lapps had dotted around their tents, and in such wonderful condition despite the climate, and she really wished she'd asked them how they managed to keep them so well . . . but she hadn't.

Mrs Lavenham searched for another question. 'What are the best conditions to grow lavender?' asked a woman in the front row.

The air-traffic controller took this, answering with the kind of excited tone and fidgety manner you always hope the man guiding your aircraft down to earth doesn't have. He seemed to have little control over his arms as he gesticulated his way through advice on sunny positions and well-drained soil, reminding the questioner to prune old bushes in the spring and even suggesting that she grow rosemary in the same bed. 'They do well together and the scent is divine.'

He blushed as he got a little round of applause for his efforts. Mrs Lavenham thanked him and then glanced my way, as if to warn me: your turn next.

Walters raised his hand. I wasn't sure if this was good or bad. He wouldn't ask anything about plants; he'd want to know if the panel had an opinion on the use of napalm or suchlike in the garden. But then a man nearer the back caught Mrs Lavenham's eye and she gave him the floor.

'I'd like to ask the panel about ornamental grasses,' he said.

I didn't hear anything after that. My brain had tripped out, overloading on the surge of desperation the two words 'ornamental' and 'grasses' had produced. I found myself floating above the room, drifting through memories of a family holiday to Brittany long ago when all I had to do was get up and go to the beach and spend the day in the sea and on the sand and eating ice creams, with no responsibilities, no fear and no thought of tomorrow. I came to as he said, '. . .the incomparable joys of a pampas grass.' And then he stopped, waiting for an answer.

Mrs Lavenham turned to me. I felt sweat dribble down my back. I leant forward on my elbows for effect. I sucked through my teeth, for more effect. I was all effect. I looked round at each of my clients. Annie Kendal gave me a feisty look back: you tell him what to do with his ornamental grasses. Nugent rolled his eyes with a: well I know what I'd do with ornamental grasses. While Sweeney had a face that said: who gives a toss about ornamental grasses?

'Ornamental grasses,' I said, and felt the audience stiffen in expectation. 'Well . . . I could go on all night about ornamental grasses . . . but, instead, I'm going to pass this question on to my colleague who has just returned from South America, the spiritual home of grasses.' And I turned and smiled at the orchid expert, who sat up like a puppy dog. 'Ah . . .' he sighed, 'I don't think I'll ever see another ornamental grass without thinking of Patagonia,' and he was off.

I got away with that one, and it occurred to me that this was the best way to survive the evening: by dodging questions rather than trying to answer them. My reputation would be damaged beyond redemption, but, if I deflected questions to the more eager and better informed folk around me, at least I could save myself from ending up under the table in a pool of embarrassment. My next question came from a Welsh woman who wanted to know the secret of good compost. 'I could happily talk all night about compost,' I replied, 'but we are fortunate to have in the audience tonight a composter par excellence, Mr Nugent from Tufnell Park, who I'm sure would be only too pleased to . . .' and before I could say 'answer your question', Nugent was answering her question.

For the next two hours I managed to expertly avoid a range of questions concerning water gardens, ferns, rockeries and potato blight. For anything technical I turned to the panel. For things more domestic I turned to my clients in the audience. Annie Kendal answered a question on what to do if your child has eaten a tulip; Walters answered one on how to get rid of slugs, suggesting torture was as good a method as any. How I longed for someone to ask what the best way to rake up leaves was, or how to weed out a dandelion so it felt no pain, so that I too could show I had a field of expertise. But it wasn't to be. To begin with everyone assumed I was simply being generous in the way I passed round my questions. Then after a while they suspected I was, perhaps, short on detail. By the time the evening drew to a close they realised I knew little or nothing. The only question I answered on my own was when Helen put her hand up.

'I'd just like to ask the panel if they can recommend any music or musician to listen to while gardening.'

Such an off-beat question caught the others off guard, enabling me to jump right in. 'Good question,' I said. 'It could depend on the weather of course, and on the time of year, but I generally find you can't go wrong with Elvis Costello.'

'Good,' she said. 'Thank you.'

'You're welcome.'

There was time for one last question. Bernie had his hand up. 'Now that winter is here,' he said, 'should we be tempted just to ignore the garden, or should we be working hard in preparation for next year?'

He was, of course, trying to drum up business for his nursery, but Mrs Lavenham didn't need any encouragement on this matter and she decided to answer herself. She said, 'I would go so far as to say that the work you do in the winter is as important as the work in the summer. Everything you do now, from protecting plants from the frost, to cleaning the windows of the greenhouse to allow more light in during the short days, is going to pay dividends come the flowering season. Now is the time to plan, to redesign, to rethink. The garden may be hibernating, but a good gardener certainly isn't.'

She spoke with such conviction and with an air of such

wisdom that it sounded like a warning to all those stupid enough to ignore her. The audience remained silent for a moment, as if they'd been found out. Then Bernie started to applaud and the rest followed, and the evening closed with the crowd emboldened as if they'd been called to arms.

I'd had my eye on the fire exit for some time, and now I backed away from the platform to make an escape. Having revealed myself as a fraud all I wanted to do was get out of this hall, out of Hampstead and out of gardening for good. But the long willowy arms of Mrs Lavenham caught me and led me back for more mulled wine. 'I'm sorry about my performance,' I said.

'Wasn't your fault! Every time you went to answer a question, someone stole it off you.'

'They did, didn't they.'

Someone was tapping me on the shoulder. I turned to see Major Chesney. I really thought he was going to hit me with his walking stick, or, worse, ask for my wages back, but to my disbelief he said, 'I hope you're going to keep coming to me throughout the winter.' I looked into his bloodshot eyes. Either he was very drunk, or he had a cruel sense of humour. 'I had a dream not so long ago,' he said. 'The lawn was so smooth I was playing bowls on it. Think you could manage that?'

'I'm not sure.'

'Good.'

Then Kenneth was next to me. He handed me a glass of wine and said, 'I want you to come round and have lunch and we'll talk about bulbs. How about Wednesday next week?'

'He comes to me on a Wednesday,' said Lady Brignal, elbowing her way through. She pointed her fine bones at me and said, 'And another thing. I'm going to put your rate up to £2 an hour.'

'So am I,' said Kenneth.

It was as if we had attended two separate, maybe parallel, events. In one I had been a disaster, unable to answer the simplest of questions on gardening matters, but in the other I had been a guru without whose attention flower beds would wilt and die.

When Annie Kendal came over and told me she had changed her mind, she wanted me to keep coming through the winter, I had to know the truth. 'I'm confused,' I said. 'Why ask me to be your gardener? Why not ask someone like the guy who has just come back from hunting orchids?'

'Oh, we don't want anyone like that,' she said.

'Like what?'

'A know-all. We want someone who . . .'

'Knows nothing?'

'We want someone who's . . . one of us.'

It was a moment of truth if ever there was one. All summer I had been trying to convince people that I was competent, that they could leave their gardens in my safe hands, that I had green fingers even. But it had all been unnecessary. The people who employed me didn't want an expert. They were suspicious of experts, in fact. They wanted someone to look after their garden who was like themselves, only with the time and energy to do the job. They had, after all, looked for a gardener in a newsagent's window. They hadn't sought out some horticultural maestro with letters after his name. They had chosen someone who advertised himself next to a chest of drawers for sale, someone who could muddle through.

Understanding this changed everything. I suddenly found myself acting with an honesty that was liberating. 'What do you know about ground cover?' one woman asked me.

'Nothing.'

'Maybe you'd like to come round and talk to us about it.'

'You're the boss.'

From teetering on the brink of shame, the evening turned into a job market for me. Having been told by the experts that they needed to keep their gardens in shape over the winter, everyone was now keen to employ someone to do the job who was the antithesis of an expert.

I worked my way through the hall, returning Nugent's wink as he continued to charm the Welsh woman with his compost anecdotes; nodding to Sweeney, as he stuck his finger in Major Chesney's face and lectured him on communism; overhearing Annie Kendal talking about mincemeat recipes with Mrs Lavenham, and Kenneth humming Beethoven to Joan Peek. And I felt like a reprieved man. It looked as though I wouldn't be driving a delivery van through the winter after all. Helen came up to say goodnight, and she whispered to me, 'If I had a garden I'd want you to look after it.' And for the first time I had a glimpse of a future in which I wasn't a writer, but a man of the soil. It was strangely comforting.

I turned and found myself standing next to the man who had earlier asked me about ornamental grasses. He was smirking at me now, nodding in a knowing way.

'What?' I said.

'Elvis Costello?'

'Yes, Elvis Costello.'

'What about Abba?'

'What *about* Abba?'

'When I'm turning over my beds I like to listen to Abba.'

Now I smirked at him. 'I'm sorry, but someone who listens to Abba when they're turning over beds knows very little about gardening.'

I went to the Freemason's afterwards with Neil and

Mandy, and sat there looking smug. 'I might start a company,' I said. 'I'll get myself a van and an assistant. And a clever name like Daylight Shrubbery Ltd.'

Mandy put her arm through mine and said, 'We should go into business together, you and me, a door-to-door hair-dressing and gardening company.'

'You could call yourself Roots,' said Neil

Not as crazy an idea as it sounded.

We bought a takeaway curry and went home. Neil must have plonked the cartons right on top of the letter from the BBC. I didn't find it until after we'd eaten and I was clearing up. The envelope was soaked in chicken biriani sauce, and the letter inside was stained and limp.

But I recognised the name at the bottom straight away: John Lloyd, Producer, *Not the Nine O'Clock News*. He simply said that he liked our work very much and wanted to use a sketch we'd sent him – the bank sketch – in the following week's show. We should go in to see him at the TV Centre as soon as we could.

I read it again and again. The whole evening had had a dreamlike quality and I wanted to make sure I hadn't missed out a word, some negative that could completely change the sense. But it didn't matter how many times I read it, it still smelt of curry and it still said he wanted to buy one of our sketches.

I called Dick. He tried to be calm about it, but then announced he was going out first thing to buy that yellow and brown suit he'd seen on a stall in Walthamstow market, and I knew how excited he was. He asked, 'Does he mention money?'

'No.'

'Good. Let me handle the negotiations.'

We went in to the BBC the next day. John Lloyd immediately took us to the BBC Club bar, a very sociable place with a sticky carpet where comedy producers drank too much and threatened to throw each other out of the window and onto the Blue Peter garden four floors below.

He said he wanted to use two sketches: the bank sketch and a quickie about the man from the Michelin Guide who sits in the corner of a restaurant wearing tyres.

'How much?' said Dick.

'£60 for the two.'

'£120,' came back Dick – putting into play his clever plan to ask for twice as much as was offered.

'£60,' said John Lloyd.

'It's a deal,' said Dick.

As we left, John said he'd like to see anything else we cared to send him. It was the remark that made nine months' effort feel worthwhile.

That evening we celebrated in an Italian restaurant. We drank a lot of red wine and talked loudly about how the future of comedy was in our hands.

Dick said, 'You're no longer a gardener who writes comedy. You're a comedy writer who works as a gardener now and again.'

'You're right. So are you.'

'What?'

'What you just said.'

'I'm not a gardener?'

'I know you're not. Neither am I.'

It was a day we would always remember. Unfortunately, five thousand miles away, a lone man with a gun was about to make sure it was a day millions of other people would remember as well.

20

JOHN LENNON

When the phone went early the next morning I knew it was Mr Gold. He said, 'Got a little job for you in Kentish Town.' One of his tenants had been digging in the garden and come across a pile of bones. 'She's a bit hysterical,' said Gold. I wasn't thrilled about it myself, but he assured me it was probably just someone's pet cat, and asked could I go round and deal with it.

'OK,' I said. And there was a pause and then he said, 'I suppose you've heard the news?'

The morning was cold and wet as I cycled down the Finchley Road. But it was events in New York that made me feel numb: John Lennon shot dead in the street.

People walked with heads down. Bus conductors collected money in silence. Every car radio was playing a Lennon song. A cloud of disbelief hung over the city. I freewheeled along, hoping each bump would wake me from a dream.

The tenant of Gold's flat seemed to be the only person in London who hadn't heard, and then when I told her she was the only person who wasn't bothered. 'I'm a Cliff fan,' she said.

She pointed me towards the garden. She wouldn't come down the path with me. 'I was planting daffodils,' she said. 'And there was this skull. I didn't move here to find dead bodies,' and she shivered and ran inside.

I found the patch she was digging. It was a rabbit, that was all. Gold was presumably right – a pet, buried long ago. I dug the bed over and collected all the bones in a bin liner. I was about to pack up when one last dig produced another bone, but this was different, bigger. I dug further and found more. And then another skull emerged, a dog's by the look of it, another pet, only this one had the collar still on and a rusty nameplate: Ivanhoe.

How old was Ivanhoe? Was it worth carbon-dating him? I shovelled his bones into the bin liner and dug on.

Next to Ivanhoe was a cat, then a rodent sort of creature, a hamster perhaps. This was getting sick. I had struck a pet cemetery, or worse – the victims of a pet serial killer.

After an hour I'd had enough. I was also getting frightened that the next corpse would be the pets' owner. I cycled back up to Hampstead and showed what I had found to Gold. He was appalled. 'What have we done?' he said. The idea of disturbing a burial ground made him pale.

'There's only one thing we can do,' he said softly, and he took me down in the lift and led me out into the communal garden.

Sleet began to fall as we buried the bones under a rhododendron. Gold bowed his head and joined his hands and may even have said a few words under his breath. I stood there solemnly, wondering if he was going to pay me extra for all this.

*   *   *

I wanted to find Helen and tell her about our success with *Not the Nine O'Clock News*, but the day was so strange, so sad, that it was hard to feel good about anything. I pulled up my hood and pushed my bike along the wet pavements. I saw the Powerflowers van and went and told Don I didn't want his job. He didn't sneer at me in his threatening way; he didn't even look like he wanted to hit me. He just mumbled, 'Suit yourself mate,' and wound the window up. One of his crew said to me, 'Don't worry about him; he's a bit upset about . . . you know.'

As I got to Lady Brignal's house I could hear John Lennon's music coming from an upstairs room. Helen opened the door to me and before I knew it she'd thrown her arms around me. I was so surprised I stood there like a plank.

'It's just dreadful,' she whispered. She had baggy eyes and a sore nose. This was going to be a difficult time for a lot of people our age. It would take a while just to sink in. It was like a death in the family.

We took Byron for a walk on Parliament Hill. The clouds hurtled across the sky, the daylight already on the downward curve. Without leaves on the trees you could see from one side of the Heath to the other. Winter had turned it black and white, and we had it all to ourselves. The sleet came again and we huddled together on a bench. She said, 'I need cheering up.'

I took a breath and told her, 'We've sold two sketches to *Not the Nine O'Clock News*.'

'You're kidding!'

'No.'

'That's wonderful! Just wonderful!' And she hugged me once more, and this time I was ready for it.

We went to the café in the Royal Free Hospital again, and she insisted on buying me a Bakewell tart. 'Happy

Christmas (War is Over)' was playing on the radio in a non-stop John Lennon tribute. The Beatles had provided the soundtrack to our youth, and now it felt as if that was all over and done with. 'I feel like a grown-up,' I said.

Helen tried to smile. She knew I wanted to be happy with my success. She said, 'It's the end of something, but . . . it's also a beginning. You've got your break. There's no looking back now.'

The way she leaned across the table and spoke to me, it was impossible not to feel invincible. She was right: one adventure was coming to a close, but a new one was starting, right here in this waiting room, surrounded by people with bandages and crutches.

'I have just one piece of advice,' she said.

'What's that?'

'Don't give up the day job.'

Travels with Boogie

Mark Wallington

Classic humour in the English countryside – *500-Mile Walkies* and *Boogie Up the River* now in one volume.

Travels with Boogie is the story of two city slickers – one an unattractive but streetwise mongrel from Stockwell, the other the long-suffering author – and how they came to terms with England's countryside and waterways.

First they had to survive against all odds as they embarked on a heroic journey up hill and down dale, with rucksacks full of Kennomeat, along Britain's longest coastal footpath – from Somerset to Devon, from Cornwall to Dorset. And they did it. Then, undaunted, they took on the treacherous waters of the Thames. Not exactly as Mark had planned, however: this time his companion was to be the delectable Jennifer – but she was held up at the office, and when Boogie was dropped off at the kennels the other dogs complained.

Travels with Boogie is a witty and fascinating account of a mismatched couple and of the people they meet and places they visit.

'The humorous travel book we've been waiting for' *Daily Mail*

arrow books